Military 2 Civilian Employment

Explore other innovative resources by CERIC:

Career Development in 2040: "Preparing for Possible Scenarios of Work & Careers" and "10 Major Changes Impacting the Futures of Work and Workers in Canada"

Computing Careers & Disciplines: A Quick Guide for Prospective Students and Career Advisors

Practice Principles: Career Theories and Models at Work

Retain and Gain: Career Management for the Public Sector Playbook. Small Business and Non-profit editions also available

Strengthening Mental Health Through Effective Career Development: A Practitioner's Guide

Career Work in Action: Discussions and Activities for Professionals

Military 2 Civilian Employment

A Career Practitioner's Guide
2nd Edition

Yvonne Rodney

CERIC

Published and distributed in 2025 by
CERIC
2 St. Clair Avenue East, Suite 300
Toronto, Ontario, Canada M4T 2T5
Tel: (416) 929-2510
https://www.ceric.ca

Library and Archives Canada Cataloguing in Publication

Rodney, Yvonne
Military 2 Civilian Employment: A Career Practitioner's Guide 2nd Edition / Yvonne Rodney.

ISBN
Print book ISBN: 978-1-988066-88-2
eBook ISBN: 978-1-988066-89-9
ePDF ISBN: 978-1-988066-90-5

Book Design: Authority Pilot
https://authoritypilot.com

In memory of Dr. Rob Shea, whose dedication to the military community and the field of career development has left a lasting legacy. As a CERIC Board member and an ardent supporter of veterans, Rob's vision was instrumental in the creation of this guide. His leadership and insights have resulted in an essential resource for Canada's career practitioners, ensuring that those who have served can transition smoothly into civilian life. This second edition is a testament to his enduring impact and his passion for helping others find their way.

Rob, thank you for leading the way; your work continues to inspire and empower.

Contents

From the Publisher

Canadian career professionals working with ex-military clients across Canada need an up-to-date specialized resource to help their clients smoothly transition from military roles into the civilian workforce. As a national charitable organization that supports the development of resources to enhance the work of Canadian career professionals, CERIC first recognized the importance of meeting this need a decade ago. The result was *Military to Civilian Employment: A Career Practitioner's Guide*, a resource launched in 2016, in both English and French. The demand for support with employment transition for Veterans has remained high. Now, there are more than 450,000 Veterans in Canada (between the ages of 17 and 59). Each year across the country, approximately 8,200 military members are released from Regular Force and Reserve Force and increasingly at a younger age.

In the time since CERIC began to develop the first edition of the book, our organization has continued to support military transitions. Likewise, we have continued to hear from career professionals across Canada about the challenges that clients with military backgrounds are facing. Given these evolving circumstances, it became essential to provide an updated resource that reflected changes in the military ecosystem and would help career professionals and their clients navigate the complexity of a new reality (one shaped by a pandemic, labour and skills shortages, and international geopolitical conflicts).

This project would not have been possible without the critical support and encouragement provided by Dwayne L. Cormier and his amazing team at the Canadian Armed Forces' Military Transition Engagement and Partnerships (MTEP) unit. Their passion and commitment to increasing awareness and improving support systems for the transition process were essential for the content of this second edition.

Our special thanks to the following Knowledge Champions for their leadership in supporting the project: Athabasca University; Canadian Military, Veteran and Family Connected Campus Consortium (CMVF3C); Fanshawe College; RBC Insurance; Release Point Education; Together We Stand (TWS) Military Families Foundation; and University of Alberta. Your support ensured the development and dissemination of the guide.

The guide's author, Yvonne Rodney, again went through the process of collecting content, updating information and resources, and interviewing sources, all from a career development lens. With the support and collaboration of subject matter experts from Canadian Armed Forces, Veterans Affairs Canada, Military Family Services, CAF Veterans and their families, and front-line career professionals, she describes the complex reality of the military, translating Veterans' needs so that career development professionals can better understand and help their clients.

The continuous support of the CERIC Board of Directors was essential; they endorsed and valued the idea of a second edition. A heartfelt thank you to founding CERIC board member Dr. Rob Shea, to whose memory this book is dedicated. Rob was a long-time military supporter. Among his many roles, he served as the Newfoundland and Labrador Provincial Chair of the Canadian Forces Liaison Council, and he championed this project, not once, but twice.

Transitions can be challenging, but also full of opportunities. Transitioning from the first edition of *Military to Civilian Employment: A Career Practitioner's Guide* to this second edition was such a meaningful learning process, and we hope you find this new resource to be highly useful in your work.

With this updated guide in hand, Canada's career development professionals are better equipped to support Veterans who in turn are better able to navigate the civilian job market and workforce. It is absolutely essential that as a country we empower those who served their country to move into prosperous careers, where they can continue to contribute their knowledge, experience and resourcefulness and serve in new and meaningful ways.

— Kay Castelle, Executive Director, CERIC

From the Author

Since 2016, when the first edition of *Military to Civilian Employment: A Career Practitioner's Guide* was published, much has changed in military culture and in the resources available to support members transitioning to civilian employment. This edition attempts to capture and communicate salient information to help in working with transitioning military members, Veterans or military spouses/partners.

You will be introduced to the impressive infrastructure currently in place to support military members, Veterans and their families inclusive of the Canadian Armed Forces Transition Group (CAF TG), Veterans Affairs Canada (VAC) Military Spousal Employment Network (MSEN) and more. Hundreds of third-party organizations and service providers are at hand to assist in what now very closely approximates a one-stop, hub-and-spoke model. This is huge and long overdue!

Some of the key information from the first edition remains but has been updated, including answers to these questions: What kind of life comprises military service? Why do people join? Why do they stay? Why do they leave? And when they leave, what do they need to successfully transition to civilian employment? New to the second edition are chapters dedicated to Reservists, military cultural competent counselling, and the CAF as an employer, and interspersed throughout are new profiles, data, resources, and services.

This guide is for career practitioners who know little about life in the military. It is meant to be used as a reference book, if you will, to better understand the unique employment-related needs of former and current military members and their families who might seek your professional assistance. It is intentionally written in a collegial tone, as if we were sitting together in a comfortable room sharing good information.

I hope you find it both useful and engaging.

— Yvonne Rodney

Acknowledgements

For this iteration of *Military 2 Civilian Employment: A Career Practitioner's Guide*, I experienced first-hand the military characteristics you will read about in this book: teamwork, hard work, sharing of resources, getting the mission accomplished, and doing it right. I have been struck anew by the generosity of spirit and commitment that so characterize the CAF members and Veterans I've had the privilege of working with. These individuals graciously gave of their time and generously shared resources that contributed to the content of this book.

From the start of this project, Dwayne L. Cormier (a major facilitator in the first edition) and Jordan Camarda have been my wingmen. Committed, collegial, determined, and kind, they went to bat to get me the people and resources needed, even giving me their own work to incorporate. Sirs, I am so very grateful for you and who you are. And then they brought in Maria Relucio, who ensured my I's were dotted, T's were crossed and information was accurate. Maria knows where to find stuff!

When I naively questioned why we needed a dedicated section on Reservists, Dwayne connected me to Lieutenant-Colonel Paul Szabunio who in turn quickly pulled together a team of experts to meet with me: Major Shelly Bellise, Tom Quigley, Eleanor Taylor, and others. By the end of that hour, I had all the resources I needed to write that chapter well. So impressive!

I knew I wanted to flavour this book with testimonials of military personnel who have transitioned to civilian employment. I love stories. As with the first edition, these "profilees" did not disappoint. The details of each person's journey and the words of wisdom at the end of each profile are definitely inspiring! Caleb Walker also referred me to many people to interview for these profiles. Check out his *Cup of Joe* newsletter on LinkedIn.

True confession: I have a soft spot for military families. Vanessa Walsh, Elizabeth Nicholas, Nathalie Kirouac, and Cindy Girard-Grenier exemplify the support that Military Family Services provide. They went over and above to review, share, and direct, and had such *joie de vivre* in the giving; I wanted to become their friends! Thank you.

Elaine Piper and Sue Watts, fellow career practitioners—to you I owe a debt of gratitude for the work you do and the time you took to read, review, provide feedback and share. You wanted this book to connect with our colleagues just as much as I did and you showed it in your actions. Thanks so very much!

CERIC staff: The unflappable Alexandra Manoliu, who deftly managed this project and kept us cognizant of timelines and meeting outcomes—working with you has been a pleasure. Thanks for listening and giving me space to brainstorm; Sharon Ferriss, who makes connections happen so effortlessly, and the entire CERIC team behind the scenes who continue to champion outstanding work in career development—you are soldiers in the truest sense of the word. And to Dimitra Chronopoulos, copy editor extraordinaire whose thoroughness and attention to detail is second to none. Thank you.

Teamwork does make the dream work. Below are the titles associated with this team, in case you're curious.

- Major Shelly Bellisle – Senior Operations Officer, External Engagement, Directorate of Employer Support Programs, CAF
- Jordan Camarda – National Manager, Military Transition Engagement and Partnerships, CAF TG
- Dimitra Chronopoulos – Freelance editor
- Dwayne L. Cormier – Strategic Initiatives Manager and Transition Guru, Military Transition Engagement and Partnerships, CAF TG
- Sharon Ferriss – Senior Director, Marketing and Communications, CERIC
- Cindy Girard-Grenier – Conseillère d'orientation/Guidance Counsellor, Centre de ressources pour les familles militaires Valcartier/ Valcartier Military Family Resource Centre
- Nathalie Kirouac – Conseillère d'orientation/Guidance Counsellor, Centre de ressources pour les familles militaires Valcartier/Valcartier Military Family Resource Centre
- Alexandra Manoliu, Ph.D. – Manager, Research Initiatives, CERIC
- Elizabeth Nicholas – Trenton Military Family Resource Centre
- Elaine Piper – Military to Civilian Transition Expert and military spouse (retired)

- Tom Quigley – National Director Outreach and Alliances, The Treble Victor Group
- Maria Relucio, Ph.D., R.B.A. (Ont) – Program Support Officer, Military Transition Engagement and Partnerships, CAF TG
- Lieutenant-Colonel Paul A. Szabunio – Strategic Liaison Partner, Military Transition Engagement and Partnerships, CAF TG
- Eleanor Taylor – Community Engagement & Advocacy, True Patriot Love Foundation
- Caleb Walker – Founder/CEO, The Digital Insurgency and *Cup of Joe* newsletter
- Vanessa Walsh – Senior Manager, Military Family Services
- Sue Watts – Executive Director, Employment + Education Centre

— Yvonne

Reader's Guide

In the busyness of our work there isn't always time to read a book from cover to cover. With that in mind, this guide is written in such a way that you can start at any chapter that catches your attention. Information may be repeated in multiple places so you don't have to always go back to a previous chapter to get what you need. Here are a few quick notes to help you make the most of the reading.

Who Is the Guide about?

This book is primarily about transitioning members or Veterans of the Canadian **Regular Force** and **Reserve Force** with a section on military spouses/partners. Regular Force Veterans would have been employed full-time within the Canadian Armed Forces (CAF). Reservists are part-time soldiers who provide support to the Regular Forces domestically or internationally and typically serve (evenings/weekends) while holding down full-time civilian jobs or schooling. Reservists may also apply to serve on full-time contracts similar to those of Regular Force members.

A **Veteran**, as defined by Veterans Affairs Canada, is "any former member of the Canadian Armed Forces who successfully underwent basic training and is honourably discharged."[1]

Features of the Guide

Chapter Contents: You will be told the content of each chapter right up front.

Key Learning: Important points are listed at the end of each chapter.

Yvonne's Favourites: Resources that I find particularly useful are listed at the end of each chapter. Not all chapters have this feature.

Profiles: The experiences of real CAF service personnel and spouses provide first-hand intelligence on the transition process. Names and other personal identifiers have been changed (unless directed otherwise).

Initialisms and Acronyms: The following initialisms and acronyms are used frequently throughout the book:

CAF	Canadian Armed Forces
CAF TG	Canadian Armed Forces Transition Group
CFMWS	Canadian Forces Morale and Welfare Services
DND	Department of National Defence
MFS	Military Family Services
MTEP	Military Transition Engagement and Partnerships
NCM	non-commissioned member
VAC	Veterans Affairs Canada

The Canadian Armed Forces comprise three main environments and the Special Forces:

- **SEA – Royal Canadian Navy (RCN)** – The Navy's role is to protect Canadian sovereignty and interests at sea, at home, and abroad. It is committed to promoting global stability, enforcing international laws, and assisting in the protection of not just Canada but world economies.

- **LAND – Royal Canadian Army** – The Army, on behalf of the Government of Canada, deploys special operations forces to protect our country from threats at home or abroad.

- **AIR – Royal Canadian Air Force** (RCAF) – The Royal Canadian Air Force defends and protects Canadian and North American airspace in partnership with the United States. The RCAF also contributes to international peace and security.

- **The Special Forces** employ specifically selected, highly trained personnel who often work for sustained periods of time under difficult conditions. It is a high-readiness organization.

The "purple trades" provides support to all the environments of the CAF in the areas of healthcare, logistics, resource management, human resources, and technicians. Members in the purple trades can work within all environments regardless of uniform designation.

Useful Statistics and Information

- According to 2021 Census data, there are 261,095 Veterans aged 25 to 64 years—the key working-age time span.[2]

- Roughly 8,200 CAF members (Regular and Reserve) transition from military service annually.[3]

- Through to 2032, the Canadian Defence Team aims to grow to 71,500 Regular Force members (from 68,000) and 30,000 Reserve Force members (from 27,000).[4]

Introduction

Every year, thousands of CAF members transition from the military. Sooner or later, one of them may seek out your services or mine. Many of these members, especially those who have spent a number of years in service, have little or no experience of the civilian job market, hence a reason for this career practitioner's guide. It is meant to provide context, background, useful tools, and resources to help us work effectively with military members, Veterans, and their families in their transition to civilian life.

A career in the Canadian Armed Forces is a call to duty. The soldiers, sailors, and air personnel who through the years have answered this call exemplify many of the values that define and unite Canadians from coast to coast. They have a will to fight for and protect what they believe in and possess a desire to help others. And that commitment places service before self.

The Canadian Armed Forces (CAF) is a unique organization where members learn and develop combat and combat-support skills. Career progression, for the most part, is based on experience and knowledge acquired through training and employment within the CAF itself. It is a career like no other.

In 2017, the Department of National Defence (DND) released its most extensive and expensive consultation policy document to date, "Strong. Secure. Engaged – Canada's Defence Policy." Within that document are outlined a number of initiatives to support military members and families though all the transitions military life entails. One of these initiatives was the creation of a new 1,200-personnel Canadian Armed Forces Transition Group (CAF TG). This was launched in 2018. The purpose of the CAF TG is to "provide a fully engaged, personalized, guided support to transition all Canadian Armed Forces members, with special care and attention being provided to those who are ill or injured, including those with psychological or critical stress injuries."[5]

With the establishment of the CAF TG and a commitment within the new DND and CAF departmental plan to bring it to its full operational capability by 2024-25,[6] there are currently 27 fully operational Transition Centres across the country.[7]

Furthermore, in 2024, the National Veterans Employment Strategy was published after extensive consultations with Veterans, CAF members, employers, and both national and community-based support organizations. The overarching objectives of this Employment Strategy include improving direct support to Veterans and transitioning members, recognizing Veteran Friendly employers, improving support, and resources for those seeking careers in the public service (as many Veterans do) and building relationships and partnerships across the Veterans employment spectrum.

This guide is just one resource where you can learn about services available to transitioning CAF members and families in all domains of their well-being. Once you have completed it, you can then move on to the bigger challenge (but worth the investment of time) of discovering the wealth of supports and services available to the entire military, Veteran, and family community. Currently, the Canadian Armed Forces Transition Group's National Resource Directory has hundreds of registered organizations, and this list is growing daily, all committed to providing value-added supports and resources to military members, Veterans and their families. In addition, True Patriot Love's Veteran Hub has over 400 military friendly organizations. It is a robust and evolving network.

No way can you be expected to know, let alone retain, all this information but Dwayne L. Cormier, career practitioner to the CAF community for over two decades, offers a practical approach. Imagine you now have a Veteran sitting in front of you. Where do you begin?

A good place to start is to check and see where they are in their transition.

- Have they been connected to a CAF Transition Advisor?
- Have they participated in CAF-led Career Transition Workshops?
- Have they already left the military?
- Are they now connected to the VAC Career Transition Services program?
- Are they a year out or are they at the 30-day mark?
- What is/was their rank?
- Are they contemplating leaving the CAF because their spouse can't find a rewarding career?
- Are they a Reservist?

Different scenarios will be needed based on the different clients and the stages they are at in their transition. Our aim therefore is to help our client create an action plan, identifying the barriers or challenges to employment and then referring out, when needed, to the right specialist to provide the training/ supports to overcome those barriers/challenges.

Cormier recommends the National Resource Directory's list of verified and categorized organizations, governmental departments, third-party providers, education, and training institutes as a good place to start. Cormier says, "As you become more and more familiar with the MVF [military, Veteran, family] community and [its] supporting ecosystem, you will very quickly see that there is no shortage of supports, regardless of the path your client is on."

So let's get to it!

PART I

Military Culture

"Because of the sacrifices that our military personnel make every day, Canada remains among the safest and most secure countries in the world."

—Strong. Secure. Engaged. Canada's Defence Policy[8]

"A Matter of Serendipity + Having a Battle Buddy"

Carl spent over 35 years in the Canadian Armed Forces, gradually advancing to senior officer roles. His father served before him as a non-commissioned member, and after being invited to spend two days at the Royal Military College (RMC) playing hockey, Carl decided he wanted to serve too.

After graduating from high school, Carl applied to and was accepted to the RMC through the Regular Officer Training Plan (ROTP). Following graduation he pursued a master's degree at the recommendation of one of his RMC professors and secured a full scholarship to a public university.

"From the beginning, I had people who went to bat for me," Carl says. "I was always cognizant of those benefits." Carl has done his best to do his work with an open and consultative approach, influenced heavily by the examples of those who mentored him.

Out of uniform now for a year and a half, Carl reflects on his transition: "I was ready. For me it was a very positive, planned exit, and I woke up the next day after I had left not feeling that I'd lost my teddy bear."

Carl credits a lot of his preparation to his transition coach, Dwayne L. Cormier (his "battle buddy"), who provided good advice like: "Every day you need to find a moment to do something for yourself to prepare for your retirement." Dwayne walked him through all the phases of transition and helped him think about what he could do after service. Carl also benefited from meeting with former members who advised and provided nuggets of wisdom.

As the months rolled by, he and his "battle buddy" ticked the boxes of things that he needed to get done, including the creation of a LinkedIn profile. "Lots of the things I'm doing now are a direct result of those LinkedIn connections."

Carl notes that he had some good opportunities come his way early into his transition and his "battle buddy" helped him with tips on how to sell himself to a civilian employer. While he was unsuccessful in securing a major opportunity immediately after leaving service, on reflection, he would have gone from an extremely busy military role to an equally busy civilian one. "Maybe it's fate. But it didn't happen, and though I had a couple other opportunities, I just decided to be cautious and disciplined about giving myself a bit of time. This was supported by advice from others to be careful and methodical. I took that to heart and see that it came to be."

Carl and his wife spent some time travelling the first year out, which was healthy. Overall, he feels that his transition has been positive. "At no time did I feel 'failed by the system.'"

Carl says he now uses three lenses to guide any opportunities that come his way: (1) Do I believe in what the company is doing? (2) Can I help them or add value? (3) Do I feel positive about the people I will be working with and around? He is currently doing some advisory work, mentoring, volunteering, and looking into a full-time opportunity, but all of his decisions have been methodical and unrushed.

About the military, Carl says "I miss the interpersonal connections, the constant interactions, the international engagements/events, camaraderie, opportunities, and friends made."

His advice to transitioning members mimics what he found most useful for himself:

- ✓ Plan early, if you have that luxury.
- ✓ Budget a bit of time every workday as you move toward the end, to do transition planning. It will give you confidence.
- ✓ Become financially literate with respect to your RRSP planning.
- ✓ In your last year of service, plan to live off the equivalent of your retirement income. That will help drive your decision regarding what jobs you can take on after retirement.

✓ Disclose any service-related injuries early, even if it is not impacting your day-to-day life. You may be eligible for disability benefits post-service.

"I've been very lucky," Carl states. "I took the best advantage of the opportunities and people assigned to help me. This is how you set yourself up for a successful transition!"

CHAPTER 1

Understanding Military Life and Culture

Many civilians, inclusive of career practitioners, educators, and employers, do not understand the nature of military life, culture, and training. The Department of National Defence (DND) provides an introduction to the Canadian Armed Forces (CAF) for those wanting a brief layperson's overview.[9] What follows is an attempt to capture for you the key elements that constitute military life so that you can have a fuller understanding to aid in your work.

The CAF and the DND form the Defence Team of Canada, employing over 100,000 military and civilian employees. This is the largest federal government department and its purpose is twofold:

1. Protect Canada and Canadians from any challenges to domestic security.

2. Help to uphold Canadian values internationally as directed by the elected government.

The CAF is responsible for defending Canada, contributing to the defence of North America, and contributing to international security. DND acts as the support system for CAF operations—base services as well as operational and corporate support.

Code of Values and Ethics[10]

The military ethos affirms certain fundamental expectations of its members. Every member should expect to work in an environment where there is mutual respect, dignity, and inclusivity so they can contribute and reach their full potential. Military values include loyalty, courage, integrity, inclusion, excellence, and accountability.

Here are the stated professional expectations:

- **Duty** means having a mission-first mindset and a willingness to get the job done at the highest professional standards despite obstacles or challenges.

- **Accepting Unlimited Liability** lies at the heart of the member's professional understanding and acceptance of duty. It means one never gives in or shies away from work even if it means pushing beyond personal limits to succeed. Despite risks or hardship one works to ensure the well-being of the team and will take calculated risks without expectations of reward.

- **Fighting spirit** is willingness to take on a task no matter how challenging it may seem. It's the commitment to remain calm and demonstrate resolve even when facing adversity and to do so with the highest level of professional and ethical conduct.

- **Leadership** means making difficult decisions based on sound moral judgement even in adverse circumstances. The leader takes responsibility for their own actions and mentors, coaches and helps to develop those they lead. They are prepared to model what is expected of subordinates, embodying all aspects of the CAF's values and ethos.

- **Discipline** is critical to maintaining high professional standards, building cohesion, and achieving military objectives. While it denotes shared values and common standards, it speaks to the discipline of one's self and development of the character strength needed to cope with the demands and stresses of one's job.

- **Teamwork** is essential in building cohesion and allows the CAF to operate in a joint and integrated manner. Priority is given to maintaining a positive demeanour and using one's influence to complement and develop the diversity of talents within the team so that members feel safe and valued.

- **Readiness** means taking seriously the desire to attain and maintain high personal and professional standards inclusive of physical fitness, honest and communicative relationship with others, and balance in work and personal life.

- **Stewardship**, which is to be practised by all military leaders, ensures that subordinates are mission ready, well informed, and motivated in performing their duties. Stewards preserve the long-term health, reputation, and viability of CAF operations.

DND/CAF Senior Governance

The **Governor General**, not the Prime Minister, is the Commander-in-Chief of Canada. The Governor General is responsible for appointing the Chief of Defence Staff at the recommendation of the Prime Minister, awarding honours and badges, the presentation of Colours, approving military badges and insignias, and signing commission documents.

The **Minister of National Defence** acts as chief executive officer for the DND and manages all matters relating to national defence. This individual is a federal Cabinet Minister.

The **Associate Minister of National Defence** is responsible for defence files as instructed by the Prime Minister and ensures that CAF members have the equipment and materials needed to do their jobs. This person is also a federal Cabinet Minister.

The **Deputy Minister of National Defence** is responsible for policy, resources, interdepartmental coordination, and international defence relations.

The **Chief of Defence Staff** is the highest-ranking officer of the CAF. He or she is responsible for the overall command, instructions, control and administration of the Forces in addition to military requirements, strategies and plans.

Rank Structure

Within the CAF, there are 19 ranks and two types of soldiers: commissioned members (officers) and non-commissioned members (NCMs) (Table 1). The culture of the CAF is unapologetically hierarchical. The chain of command is the necessary spine that supports operational effectiveness and discipline. Generally, a rank denotes one's responsibility, status, and accountability. It is essential to the discipline structure of military life. The overall job of the commanding officer is to make decisions, provide directives, and support to subordinates, respect the chain of command and be accountable for the actions of subordinates. It is the job of subordinates to implement the orders issued by their commanding officer.

Commissioned Members (Officers)

Officers must be capable of commanding; developing policies, plans, and programs; training units to accomplish designated tasks; and providing the right conditions and environments for the non-commissioned members to do their jobs effectively. To become an officer one needs the required level of university education or enrollment in the Regular Officer Training Program (ROTP). Other pathways to becoming an officer exist for non-commissioned members through the University Training Plan for Non-Commissioned Members (UTPNCM)[11] and for professionals through other CAF Paid Education programs.[12]

The highest rank in the Canadian Armed Forces is the Admiral/General who serves as the Chief of Defence Staff and is appointed by the Prime Minister from the group of military members having the rank of Vice-Admiral/Lieutenant-General.

As you can see in Table 1, the Army and the Air Force both use the same naming convention to identify ranks. The Navy is different. Some ranks in the Navy do not correspond to ranks in the Army or Air Force. For example, a Captain (Navy), is three levels higher in rank than a Captain in the Air Force or Army. This puts a Captain in the Navy on the same level as a Colonel in the Army or Air Force. Navy emblems have an added "N" beside the titles of Captain or Lieutenant. (For a pictorial depiction of ranks and appointment, visit https://www.canada.ca/en/services/defence/caf/military-identity-system/rank-appointment-insignia.html.)

Non-Commissioned Members (NCMs)

NCMs are soldiers, sailors, and aviators who form the backbone of the CAF. They perform the skilled work required for all CAF operations including the welfare and well-being of troops under their care. Senior-level NCMs (often called non-commissioned officers or NCOs), regularly participate in and inform strategic-level initiatives alongside Generals and other senior commissioned officers. This segment of the CAF is divided into eight ranks, with Chief Petty Officer 1st Class (Navy) and Chief Warrant Officer (Army and Air Force) being the highest-ranking NCMs.

NCMs can apply to become officers under different commissioning programs. If accepted they are required to complete a university degree if they don't already have one. In addition, those who have attained the rank of Sergeant or one of the ranks in the Warrant Officer group and who have demonstrated strong leadership skills could be offered a commissioning from the ranks, which, if accepted, places them in the Junior Officer group of the Officer structure. This group is not required to obtain a university degree. (Note: Many NCMs have no desire to become commissioned officers. Chief Warrant or Chief Petty Officers are at the top of their field with extensive influence and span of control to effect change. Many Lieutenant-Colonels [senior commissioned officers], depending on their occupation, do not have that same level of responsibility.)

Table 1: CAF Rank Structure

Chief of Defense Staff

Navy (Black uniform)	Army (Green uniform)	Air Force (Blue uniform)
COMMISSIONED MEMBERS (OFFICERS)		
— General Officers —		
Admiral	General	General
Vice-Admiral	Lieutenant-General	Lieutenant-General
Rear-Admiral	Major-General	Major-General
Commodore	Brigadier-General	Brigadier-General
— Senior Officers —		
Captain	Colonel	Colonel
Commander	Lieutenant-Colonel	Lieutenant-Colonel
Lieutenant-Commander	Major	Major
— Junior Officers —		
Lieutenant	Captain	Captain
Sub-Lieutenant	Lieutenant	Lieutenant
Acting Sub-Lieutenant	Second Lieutenant	Second Lieutenant
— Subordinate Officers —		
Naval Cadet	Officer Cadet	Officer Cadet

Table 1: CAF Rank Structure (cont'd)

Navy (Black uniform)	Army (Green uniform)	Air Force (Blue uniform)
NON-COMMISSIONED MEMBERS		
— Senior Appointments —		
CAF Chief Warrant Officer	CAF Chief Warrant Officer	CAF Chief Warrant Officer
Chief Petty Officer	Command Chief Warrant Officer	Command Chief Warrant Officer
Formation Chief Petty Officer	Formation Chief Warrant Officer	Formation Chief Warrant Officer
— Senior Ranks —		
Chief Petty Officer 1st Class	Chief Warrant Officer	Chief Warrant Officer
Chief Petty Officer 2nd Class	Master Warrant Officer	Master Warrant Officer
Petty Officer 1st Class	Warrant Officer	Warrant Officer
Petty Officer 2nd Class	Sergeant	Sergeant
— Junior Ranks —		
Master Sailor	Master Corporal	Master Corporal
Sailor 1st Class	Corporal	Corporal
Sailor 2nd Class	Private	Aviator
Sailor 3rd Class	Private (Basic)	Aviator (Basic)

Occupations

Occupations in the military fall into 12 broad categories. Each category comprises officers and non-commissioned members and requires specific education and/or training.

The categories are as follows:

- Health Care
- Computing and Intelligence
- Safety and Emergency Services
- Administration
- Hospitality and Support
- Public Relations
- Transport and Logistics
- Combat Operations
- Engineering and Infrastructure
- Equipment and Vehicle Maintenance
- Aviation
- Naval Operations

Terms of Service

Terms of Service (TOS) contracts for the Regular Force are typically for three years but might be longer based on the need for one's skills and the duration of training required. If the CAF pays for a member's civilian education related to their occupation (e.g., to obtain a degree to become an officer or to go to college to learn a trade), the length of service will be longer—two months for every month of paid education. Members of the Reserve Forces do not have terms of service contracts but can apply to serve in full-time contract roles within the Regular Forces.

Operational Standards

The universality of service or "soldier first" principle requires that members meet basic operational standards: be fit (successfully complete fitness evaluations), be employable (able to complete the tasks for one's job), and be deployable (not have any medical or employment liability that precludes deployment). Deployment and employment go hand in hand with each a requirement for the other.

State of Readiness

With fairly short notice, a CAF member can be called upon to undertake a specific mission. This means that the member must always be in a state of readiness: to work, if the nature of the mission requires it, irregular or long shifts; to use any mode of transportation; to eat infrequently or miss meals; and to perform under extreme physical or environmental stress and even with little or no medical support. Both body and mind must therefore be in top shape at all times.

Mobility/Postings

A serving member of the CAF can expect to be posted several times during their career. The average military family moves three times more frequently than civilians do,[13] and over 9,400 CAF members are required to move to a new province, territory or country annually. A posting typically ensures that a person gets the right experience to be considered for advancement to the next rank level. While commanding officers have input into promotions, considerations occur annually at promotions boards where members compete against their peers and are evaluated based on merit for the available promotional spots.

Competencies, Mindset and Skills

All CAF members have been trained in areas of knowledge pertinent to CAF's mission. Core knowledge about the fundamentals of tactics, strategy, command and leadership, professional conduct, and civilian relations is a must for everyone. In addition, members may also become equipped with knowledge in conflict management and all the pertinent disciplines like communications arts, human resources, history, political science and the social sciences, as well as specialized knowledge in their area of expertise.

Each serving member must be able to fire and maintain a personal weapon, conduct drills, fight fires, perform first aid/CPR, communicate using radio technology, and prepare written correspondence. Figure 1 outlines the new CAF competencies and how they relate to job performance and military cultural values.

Figure 1: CAF Competencies and Values

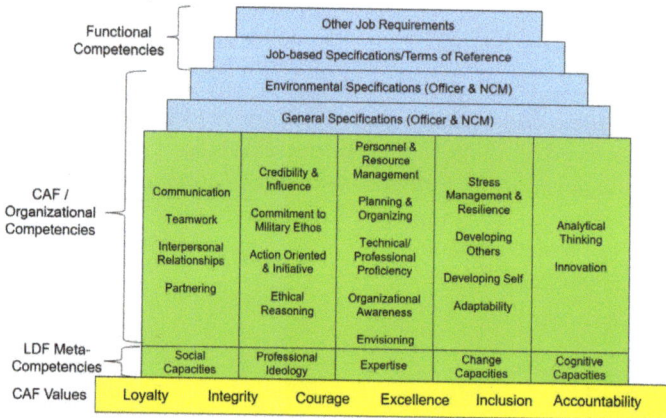

Functional Competencies	Other Job Requirements
	Job-based Specifications/Terms of Reference
	Environmental Specifications (Officer & NCM)
	General Specifications (Officer & NCM)

CAF / Organizational Competencies				
Communication	Credibility & Influence	Personnel & Resource Management	Stress Management & Resilience	Analytical Thinking
Teamwork	Commitment to Military Ethos	Planning & Organizing	Developing Others	Innovation
Interpersonal Relationships	Action Oriented & Initiative	Technical/ Professional Proficiency	Developing Self	
Partnering	Ethical Reasoning	Organizational Awareness	Adaptability	
		Envisioning		

LDF Meta-Competencies				
Social Capacities	Professional Ideology	Expertise	Change Capacities	Cognitive Capacities

CAF Values					
Loyalty	Integrity	Courage	Excellence	Inclusion	Accountability

Source: Karen J. Rankin and L. E. Noonan, Canadian Armed Forces Competency Model (CAF CM): A Framework for Application, Scientific Report DRDC-RDDC-2015-196 (Defence Research and Development Canada, 2015).

Military Schools and Training Establishments

A wide range of educational and learning opportunities are accessible once one joins the CAF. Each military member has the opportunity to establish personal learning plans whereby they can hone skills or develop new ones. However, the CAF member who is employed full-time needs to balance taking courses alongside that full-time work commitment.

The main institutions of learning associated with the Canadian Armed Forces are:

- **Royal Military College of Canada (RMC)** (https://www.rmc-cmr.ca). Located in Kingston, Ontario, RMC provides the CAF with outstanding officers ready to serve Canada. It offers undergraduate programs in the Social Sciences, Humanities, Science and Engineering in both English and French.

- **Royal Military College Saint-Jean (RMC Saint-Jean)** (www.cmrsj-rmcsj.forces.gc.ca). Companion to RMC and located in Saint-Jean-sur-Richelieu, Quebec, RMC Saint-Jean offers two college-level programs in Social Science and Science for officer and naval cadets to successfully transition from high school to university. At completion, graduates can then transfer into Year 2 at RMC.

- **Canadian Forces College (CFC)** (https://www.cfc.forces.gc.ca/221-eng.html). Located in Toronto, CFC or "Staff College" prepares senior officers in the CAF, international military members, and public- and private-sector leaders for future command roles within the global security environment of today. It provides education in the areas of defence, national security, operations, and executive leadership. It also offers a Joint Command and Staff distance-learning program.

- **Chief Warrant Officer Robert Osside Institute**. Welcoming over 3,000 students annually online and in person, Osside Institute trains senior non-commissioned members of the CAF in the competencies and knowledge required for their roles. Chief Petty Officers and Chief Warrant Officers can receive education in intermediate, advanced, and senior leadership and senior appointments areas. The Osside Institute Professional Development Program (OIPDP) allows senior Petty Officers and Warrant Officers to participate in a university-level certificate program in International Studies alongside commissioned officer and naval cadets, making it the only institution in the world where officers and non-commissioned members are trained together.

Programs for Indigenous People

The CAF offers three all-expenses-paid programs whereby Indigenous Peoples in Canada can become familiar with the CAF lifestyle.

- The **Indigenous Leadership Opportunity Year** offered through RMC Kingston welcome Indigenous participants to enrol as officer cadets for one year. The program offers individualized learning plans, leadership training, military training, sports, and cultural support activities. Students are paid at the corresponding rank level and receive free tuition and books. They can leave the program at any time.

- The **Canadian Armed Forces Indigenous Entry Program** is a three-week, hands-on experiential program that exposes Indigenous students to military training, careers, and lifestyle. Transportation, accommodation, food, clothing, and all required equipment are provided by the CAF. There is no obligation to join the CAF after completing the program.

- Five **Summer Training Programs** are offered, each lasting six weeks. The Bold Eagle, Black Bear, Carcajou, Raven, and Grey Wolf programs combine military training with Indigenous cultural teachings and help students develop self-confidence, self-discipline, teamwork, time management, respect, and fitness. While in the program, students become temporary members of the CAF, and as such, all expenses are covered. Students are also paid for the duration of their time in the program.

In addition to the above, the Military Personnel Generation Training Group (MPGTG) provides education and training for the CAF trades needed to support land, sea, and air operations. "For every single soldier in the field, pilot in the air or sailor at sea, there are seven other military members in trades supporting that operator in the field. MPGTG's job is to train those people."[14] It oversees eight training sites across the country: a chaplain school, a fire academy, a logistics training centre, a training and development centre, a leadership school, a language school, a law centre, and a conduct after capture training centre.

Training Establishments

The Army, Navy and Air Force oversee and ensure standards for their relevant training establishments. Training establishments specialize in the following and are inclusive of training provided by MPGTG:

- Aerospace studies
- Air Force selection and international training
- Armoury
- Artillery
- Basic training
- Chaplaincy
- Command

- Communication
- Engineering
- Ethics
- Foreign military training
- Infantry
- Languages
- Logistics
- Medical services
- Meteorology
- Military intelligence
- Military law
- Military training abroad
- Peace support
- Pilot training
- Policing
- Public affairs
- Search and Rescue
- Tactics

Initiatives to Achieve Change

Work is actively underway across the entire Defence Team to ensure that all members feel supported by the CAF and are able to work in an environment that fosters reaching one's highest potential. Some key areas being addressed are:

- **Sexual Misconduct** – Following a Training Needs Assessment, several recommendations are being developed to target and eliminate harmful behaviour within the CAF. Within the Sexual Misconduct and Report Centre (SMSRC), members and families affected can receive support services, participate in restorative engagement, connect with peer support teams, access legal assistance, and participate in community consultations.

- **Professional Conduct and Culture** – This plan lays out specific reporting questions leaders must answer at each reporting cycle to ensure they are meeting their goals to increase representation, inclusion, and participation of underrepresented groups across all levels of the CAF. This includes the establishment of the Chief of Professional Conduct and Culture, whose directive is to spearhead institutional efforts towards a professional conduct and culture framework that tackles all types of discrimination, harmful behaviours, biases, and systemic barriers.

- **Health and Wellness** – Over $950 million will be invested in creating new and overhauling existing health and wellness programs for Defence Team members to ensure they are able to meet professional and personal challenges. This includes the establishment of a Directorate of Women's Health within the Canadian Forces Health Services system whose job it is to oversee research specifically focused on female members, and various health-related initiatives to improve services and resources to female members. In addition, the Defence Team has released a Total Health & Wellness Strategy – a renewed and integrated approach to care for Defense Team members and their families and to promote well-being across all the domains.

- **Gender Inclusivity** – Gender-inclusive military ranks have been introduced to allow members to express their rank in a way that best matches their gender. The sex designation on military driver's licences has also been removed.

- **Inclusive Promotion and Selection Process** – Bias awareness training and a mandate that one voting member be from an equity-seeking group are two key initiatives to improve the CAF promotion and selection process.

- **Updated Nursing and Pumping Policy** – The ability to wear military-funded nursing T-shirts while in uniform, a lactation plan to support members, and inclusive practices for nursing infants are just a couple of the items covered under this policy.

- **Compassionate and Short Leave (Time Off)** – To reduce personal and family stress, CAF members will be able to request time off when tragedy strikes, for family-related situations, and even for religious/spiritual accommodation.

- **Updated Uniform and Appearance Standards** – These standards remove the barriers to choice in clothing and other areas of appearance so that the diversity of members in uniform can be honoured without compromising operational effectiveness and safety.

- **Positive Space Ambassadors** – This group promotes diversity awareness and inclusion to speak openly and positively about gender and sexual diversity, and provides assistance.

* * *

Hopefully you now have a clearer understanding of military life, culture, values, and new initiatives and how all of these shape the thinking, mindset, approach, skills, and perspectives of CAF members as they transition to civilian life and employment.

In the next chapter, we will learn more about the Reserve Force and its component parts, the competencies of its members, and the resources available to employers and Reservists alike.

KEY LEARNING

★ Military culture is committed to high professional standards and a code of conduct.

★ A member's priority is first to the mission and last to self.

★ A range of training opportunities are available within the CAF.

★ Competencies and qualities required to serve within the CAF are many and can be leveraged for civilian employment.

★ New initiatives are in place to create a more inclusive and ready CAF.

CHAPTER 2

CAF Reservists

In addition to the CAF Regular Force, there is a CAF Reserve Force. Culturally and characteristically, there are unique elements of the Reserve Force that are worth knowing and understanding. Unlike Regular Force members who are obligated to go where sent, Reservists have more latitude to volunteer for deployments or training.

Groups within the Reserve Force

Canada's Reserve Force is comprised of 28,500 members across the country. Its membership jurisdiction includes the following four groups:

The Primary Reserve (Sea, Land, Air and Special Operations)

Trained to the same standards as their Regular Force counterparts, Reservists have the opportunity of working part-time for the CAF. Many members of the Reserves hold full-time civilian jobs or attend school. Upon completion of their basic-occupation training, Reservists work or receive training through varying schedules and models depending on their element of service. Each element has a minimum time and annual skill maintenance requirement to ensure operational effectiveness. Reserve Force salaries are between 85% and 92% of Regular Force salaries with the majority of trades at 92%.[15] This also includes a reasonable benefit package. Reservists deployed on domestic or foreign operations receive identical pay and benefits to their Regular Force compatriots. Reservists on Operational Deployment (e.g., military operations abroad, select domestic operations, etc.) must quickly and seamlessly integrate with their Regular Force counterparts into a cohesive and highly capable combined force. Thus, their training and readiness must be in top form at all times. To join the Reserves, one must be at least 16 years old (with parental consent) and have completed Grade 10 (Secondaire IV) or equivalent.

Cadet Organizations Administration and Training Service (COATS)

This group is a subcomponent of the Reserve Force and is responsible for the administration, supervision and training work associated with the Cadets and the Junior Canadian Rangers, which are among Canada's largest youth leadership and engagement programs. The Cadet Instructor Cadre, made up of 7,500 members, provide this training and support, making them the largest training unit within the CAF.

The Canadian Rangers

Always ready for service, the Rangers provide military support in remote or rural communities across Canada. There are approximately 5,000 Canadian Rangers serving in 200 different communities. Rangers can get up to 12 days pay in a given year in addition to any other CAF tasks for which they have been asked to perform. They are considered "on duty" during training as well as when they are called on during an emergency or a domestic operation. Unlike their other CAF counterparts, Rangers elect their patrol leaders. To become a Canadian Ranger one must: be a Canadian citizen, be at least 18 years old, be deemed physically and mentally fit to perform Ranger duties as determined by the commanding officer, have not been convicted of a serious offence without pardon, and not a member of any other subcomponent of the CAF or affiliate organization that would conflict with the duties required of a Ranger.

The Supplementary Reserve

Managed by Commander, Military Personnel Command, the Supplementary Reserve is comprised of CAF members who have previously served in the Regular Force or another sub-component of the Reserve Force, or did not have previous military experience when they enrolled but have special skills or expertise for which there is a military requirement. The purpose of the Supplementary Reserve is to augment the Regular Force and the other sub-components of the Reserve Force. The Supplementary Reserve has about

6,700 of members. Members of the Supplementary Reserve Force are not required to undertake military training or duty unless they voluntarily transfer or are placed on active service, in times of national emergency.

In case you are wondering how this information can help you as a career practitioner working with members of the Reserves, remember the objective of this guide—to increase knowledge and understanding. From a personal perspective, I did not know the nature and rigour of training required of Reserve Force members. Nor was I familiar with the level and scope of responsibilities they may possess. Reservists are not just part-time military; they are extremely well trained and are able, when required, to quickly and effectively integrate in a Regular Force unit for short durations.

Competencies

Reservists are developed and trained to have a strong work ethic; to be mission focused, dependable, adaptable, and physically and mentally fit; and to exemplify professional conduct, responsibility, and accountability. All Reservists have experience working within teams, in either a leadership or member role, and to that end have a good understanding of how one's role contributes to operational effectiveness. Many are adept in leadership and administrative management, from budgeting and supply chain management to risk management and team building. And because they have been trained in additional areas, such as ethics, conflict resolution, planning and project management, anti-harassment, handling hazardous materials, occupational health and safety, security, first aid and more, they are well equipped to bring this knowledge and expertise to a civilian workplace.

Many Reservists are unique in that they use their military skills and experiences to enhance their civilian occupations and conversely use their civilian skills and experiences to augment their military service. Reservists truly are at the nexus between the military and civilian worlds.

Armed with this knowledge about Reservists, we as career practitioners can be more effective in helping them articulate what they bring to the table. We can ask better questions and help them document skills they may take for granted.

Job Opportunities for Reservists

As noted previously, part-time work in the Reserves develops leadership, teaches resourcefulness, and provides a wealth of marketing and transferable skills in communication, teamwork, time management, training, problem solving, and strategy planning, to name just a few.

Opportunities for Reservists in the CAF include a wide range trades and specialties in the same categories as their Regular Force counterparts:

- Health Care
- Computing and Intelligence
- Safety and Emergency Services
- Administration
- Hospitality and Support
- Public Relations
- Transport and Logistics
- Combat Operations
- Engineering and Infrastructure
- Equipment and Vehicle Maintenance
- Aviation
- Naval Operations

Employment Needs

One would assume that in terms of civilian employment, Reservists would not experience the same transitioning difficulties as members of the Regular Force since they never left the civilian world. But there is more to the Reservist employment landscape than meets the eye. According to Tom Quigley of the Treble Victor Group, Reservists face an additional burden when civilian employers assume that the duties of Reserve service will conflict with their ability to do the work for which they are employed. This perceived "liability" could impact an employer's decision to hire a Reservist in the first place because the Employment Standards Act prevents employers from denying leave requests if an employee is deployed by the CAF (inside or outside of Canada) or is participating in military skills training or related duties. In other words, if the employer does not hire the Reservist, then they are not stuck with a duty to release.

Furthermore, some Reservists have long periods of full-time service or even a full career serving in the CAF. These individuals, who might have never held *any* prior civilian role, will experience the same level of civilian adjustment and need as much support as their long-serving Regular Forces counterparts; they too will have to adapt to new cultural norms, identities, and expectations in the civilian workforce, some of which are anathema to what they have learned in the "mission first, then team, and self last" concept of military priorities. Whether Regular or Reserve Force, culturally, many transitioning members struggle with the concept of there being no "I" in TEAM, and the need for greater self-advocacy in civilian employment settings.

Support Programs

There are a myriad of programs that are open to both Regular Force and Reservists. The first access point for members and their families as they plan for their transition out of the military is the **Canadian Forces Transition Centre**. There they will be provided with personalized, professional, and standardized transition support services across multiple domains of well-being. This includes their health, finances, social integration, housing and physical environment, peer supports, sense of purpose, and cultural/societal integration. Members and their families will also be connected with **VAC**, where they will be provided with information, guidance, and support throughout the transition process and beyond.

Below is a list of some of the key supports for members and their families as they go through the transition process: (See Chapter 12 for a more comprehensive listing).

Military Transition Engagement and Partnerships (MTEP)

https://www.canada.ca/en/department-national-de-fence/services/benefits-military/transition/mtep.html

MTEP is a digital national network for organizations, businesses, and programs that support transitioning military/Veterans and their families. They work in partnership with Veterans Affairs Canada (VAC), Chief of Reserves and Employer Support (CRES), Canadian Forces Morale and Welfare Services (CFMWS), Military Family Services (MFS), and other government entities. To be considered, organizations can submit their details and an MTEP advisor will work with them to consider their application. MTEP also maintains the **National Resource Directory** (https://military-transition.canada.ca/en/national-resource-directory), where transitioning members can search a range of resources by province, domain of well-being, and populations served.

Veterans Affairs Canada (VAC) Career Transition Services

https://www.veterans.gc.ca/en/education-and-jobs/find-new-job/career-transition-services

Veterans Affairs Canada has enhanced its Career Transition Services to provide a more comprehensive support system for qualifying and still-serving Canadian Armed Forces members, Veterans, spouses/partners, and survivors. These enhanced services include one-on-one career counseling, resume writing assistance, interview preparation, labour market information, and job search support. Additionally, Veterans Affairs Canada has developed partnerships with employers and organizations to facilitate interviews and networking opportunities for Veterans. The National Veterans Employment Strategy, launched in 2024, is committed to ensuring that every Veteran finds a rewarding career after service.[16]

Chief Reserves and Employer Support (CRES) – Supporting Reservists

https://www.canada.ca/en/department-national-defence/services/canada-reserve-force/supporting-reservists.html

This web page includes information for employers and educators, and details about the following services:

- With Glowing Hearts – Reservist Support Initiative

  ○ This initiative symbolizes the commitment of select employers to attract and retain talented Reserve employees by demonstrating flexibility so that they may balance work and military commitments. This initiative highlights their support of Reservists and welcomes the skills and talents they bring to the workplace.

- Compensation for Employers of Reservists Program (CERP)

  ○ This unique CAF program reduces conflict between employers and Reservist-employees by compensating employers for the time missed by their Reservist-employees when called to serve. The program, available to civilian employers and to self-employed Reservists, helps to offset operational costs due to the absence of a Reservist-employee for military duties. Applicants may receive a lump-sum grant once the Reservist returns to work, following an absence of 30 days or more.

- ○ Qualifying criteria are as follows:

  - ✓ The civilian employer must be a Canadian employer of a Reservist-employee who is a member of the Primary Reserves or Canadian Rangers.

  - ✓ The employee's leave must be for a minimum of 30 days and the nature of the leave must be to participate in military skills training and related activities.

  - ✓ The employer must submit a complete Grant Application Package along with supporting documents no later than 12 months after the Reservist returns to work.

  - ✓ Self-employed Reservists must provide documentation to prove that their business is active and constituted their main source of employment for three consecutive months prior to the leave for military duties.

True Patriot Love Foundation

https://truepatriotlove.com/

In partnership with Veterans Affairs Canada, CAF TG, CFMWS, and a host of corporate employers, True Patriot Love is spearheading research and reporting on a number of best practices to build a more Veteran-friendly Canada. They actively champion to the employer community the unique qualities and skill sets Reservists bring to the workplace. True Patriot Love supports the entire CAF community by funding programs, facilitating collaborations, supporting research, and advocating for policy creation and changes.

Treble Victor Group

https://treblevictor.org/

Treble Victor is one of Canada's leading Veteran employment-advocacy organizations. Its mission is to enable ex-military personnel to achieve their full potential in post-service careers through common values, mutual support, teamwork, mentorship, and the network's connectivity.

Reservist Leave

Reservist Leave in Labour Codes

The CAF has been working for many years with the federal government and all provinces to include some level of Reservist Leave in their labour codes. This is protected leave in the same category as Bereavement or Family Leave. Links to the relevant portions of each labour code are as follows:

- Federal Jurisdiction: Canada Labour Code (Division XV.2)
- British Columbia: Employment Standards Act (Section 52.2)
- Alberta: Employment Standards Code (Section 53.2, page 37)
- Saskatchewan: Saskatchewan Employment Act (Section 2-53, page 39)
- Manitoba: Employment Standards Code (Section 59.5)
- Ontario: Employment Standards Act (Section 50.2)
- Quebec: Act Respecting Labour Standards (Section 81.17)
- New Brunswick: Employment Standards Act (Section 44.031)
- Nova Scotia: Labour Standards Code (Section 60H, page 46)
- Prince Edward Island: Employment Standards Act (Section 23.1, page 39)
- Newfoundland and Labrador: Labour Standards Act (Part VII.4)
- Nunavut: Labour Standards Act (Part V.2, page 22)
- Northwest Territories: Employment Standards Act (Section 32, page 40)
- Yukon: Employment Standards Act (Section 60.50, page 42)

What You Should Know about Leave Requests

If you have clients who are serving in the Reserve Force, here are some useful tips to know regarding leave requests:

- There is no need for a Reservist-employee to quit their job to serve on deployment.
- Preparation is the key when approaching an employer with a request for leave.

- The notice period for a leave of absence varies from one employer to another and can range anywhere from one to three months in advance of the leave date. Know your employer policies.

- Sample letters requesting time off to serve can be found on the DND website.[17]

- Reservist-employees should ask if they will be returning to the same civilian job or an equivalent once their time of service is completed.

- Those requesting leave from a university or college should check their institution's policy regarding delaying the completion of their program of study if called to serve.

Expanded Role of Reservists

In "A New Vision for the Reserve Force," it is explicitly outlined that fundamental change needs to happen within the Reserve Force in order to meet the demands placed on Canada's Defence Team in executing its mission.[18] This calls for the building of a stronger and more operationally ready Reserve Force that can be mobilized as needed.

Four strategy objectives have been identified to enable this expanded capability:

1. **Engage and retain** a generation of highly skilled, flexible, and operationally ready Reservists. This includes ramping up the membership by 1,500, guaranteeing four summers of paid work for each Reservist, and using those with specialized skills to fill components of the CAF cyber force.

2. **Design and implement** new and enhanced roles for Reservists, Reserve Force units and formations. Through strategic recruitment, marketing, job creation, and other initiatives, the objective is to have *all* sections of Reserve membership more fully integrated and ready to assume expanded assignments when and if required.

3. **Modernize career and socioeconomic policies**. This includes providing attractive benefits and remuneration, job protection legislation, and agile systems that allow for flexibility of movement from Reserve to Regular and back again.

4. **Design and implement** a model for fully integrating this expanded Reserve Force within the total CAF team.

Reservists as Advocates

According to Lieutenant-Colonel (Retired) Eleanor Taylor, Manager of Community Engagement and Advocacy with True Patriot Love Foundation, Reservists are the "live" connection between the CAF and the civilian world. By the very fact that they toggle between these two environments, they are uniquely positioned to demonstrate the stellar qualities and skills CAF Veterans can bring to the civilian workplace. With their well-developed leadership, teamwork, and mission-focus skills; their adaptability and agility; and their communication and general knowledge aptitudes, they are walking testimonials that can aid in deconstructing employer myths and misperceptions of military members and Veterans. Reservists can also, by the gratitude shown to employers for making time for them to serve their country, further cement the impression that "these are good people."

More Champions Needed

The CAF Directorate of Employer Support Programs office provides opportunities for civilian executives to be educated in and to experience the high level of training that is invested in each Reservist. Executives who participate are very impressed and eager to find ways to integrate Reservists within their workplaces. This type of "show," when correlated to the narrative "tell" approach, is gaining traction and momentum. Without employers hiring Reservists and retaining jobs for them, many will leave the Force and this will impact the CAF's ability to adequately defend our civil liberties. Career practitioners as a group can ask to be invited to these events. Then, having seen for themselves what impressed these executives, they too can become champions and influencers for Reservists and Veterans alike.

* * *

Now let's move to the next chapter, where we explore the employment needs of transitioning military members and Veterans.

★ The Reserve Force is diverse and highly trained.

★ Employers who see hiring of Reservists as a liability may not be aware of all they have to offer.

★ Reservists, being at the nexus of the military and civilian worlds, can be ambassadors for military transition and values.

★ Compensation is available for qualified employers who grant leave to Reservists. Application packages are available.

★ Leave for Reservists exist in all Canadian labour codes, federal and provincial.

★ Sample leave requests letters to employers are available for Reservists and Commanding Officers to use.

"That Military Guy"

The military life has always fascinated Marcel. Influenced in part by American family members who served their country, the opportunity to serve Canada was something he desired so he signed up. It became a huge part of his life, and everyone in his small eastern Canada community knew him as That Military Guy.

When faced with the decision of going to university and seeking a career path, the military seemed a safe bet, especially for someone from a large family that had no funds to send him to university. The fact that he could work in the Reserves and use that to help pay for school was an added incentive to join.

Starting out in 2012 as a lowly Private in the Infantry Reserve Force, Marcel was able to complete his university degree while in the Reserves and after graduation, signed up for a full-time Class B contract. He's served in Ukraine, Latvia, the Arctic, and really enjoyed that deployment aspect of military life. His longest stint was 5-6 years working full-time in the CAF.

Marcel's decision to leave the Reserves for good was twofold: (1) He just didn't have the time. At the rank level of Sergeant to which he'd progressed, he needed to work every weekend while putting in 60 hours per week in his civilian job. There was no work-life balance. (2) He was developing a growing frustration with military life, and a dressing down from his commanding officer when he announced his plans to leave was the last straw.

Marcel reports not availing himself of any of the transition services when he left, nor does he recall being offered any advice. He reports being told to come in to sign his release papers and that was it. He admits to feeling very jaded by then, and this lack of acknowledgement underscored why it was time to go. He was told that if he kept his cap badge, which he was led to believe each person could keep, it would be declared lost and he would be charged for it.

Because he never fully left the civilian world, transitioning out of the military was not very difficult in terms of adjusting to civilian life. Marcel's degree in Religious Studies and Business, along with the leadership training and skills military service provided, gave him the required competencies to secure a full-time recruiter role with a tech company. A year later he became an account manager and stayed with that company for three years. Currently, Marcel is working in governmental affairs in Ottawa. He loves the work and feels very supported.

In terms of adjusting to civilian work culture, Marcel reflects that it was both easy and hard. Hard in that the moniker of That Military Guy captured how much of his identity was tied to the Army. He recalls the first Remembrance Day service he attended not in uniform, after being an active uniformed participant for 14 years—"that kinda hit me in a weird way." On the other hand, returning to a world he had never quite left meant there was no culture shock to contend with.

When asked what advice he'd give those looking to transition from the military to civilian life and work, Marcel offers these words:

- ✓ The organization will survive without you. "Service before self" makes it hard to think about yourself first, but the military will make do. They will find a way to continue. As long as you're there, the military will use you. At one point you have to take a step back and think about yourself first. But the machine goes on.
- ✓ Make civilian connections long before you leave.
- ✓ You've faced tough challenges before while in service. Transition is another challenge that has to be overcome.

Marcel recommends that career practitioners and service providers resist the default assumption that all Veterans have PTSD and should be handled gingerly. Eighty percent of Veterans never access Veteran Affairs benefits, and many of those who do find what they are looking for, even if the process is cumbersome. "Approach each Veteran at face value. Not as a walking wounded. Level with them as humans. Not victims. Remind them that they have faced tough challenges while in service and that transitioning out is another challenge where they can leverage their previously demonstrated strength and training."

CHAPTER 3

Understanding the Needs

The Decision to Leave

Transitioning out of military service can happen after the member has completed their terms of service, according to their contract. However, a release can be granted prior to the end of the contract in some circumstances, if requested. The compulsory retirement age for members of the Canadian Armed Forces (CAF) is 60 years old. However, the Chief of the Defence Staff (CDS) has the discretion to authorize service beyond this age in certain cases.

The main reasons CAF Veterans voluntarily leave service, if not at retirement, stem primarily from these areas:[19]

- **Geographic stability** – Military service can take a toll on family needs. Children are impacted when they have to frequently change schools and when friends and supports are left behind and have to be re-made. How about when health care providers are no longer nearby? As noted in Simone's profile (see page 149), the multiple moves and deployments that constitute military life can be challenging for families.

- **Impact of military life on spouses/partners** – There may come a time when the non-serving partner has had enough of the military lifestyle because of how it is impacting their own career development or mental wellbeing.

- **Career management/Job Dissatisfaction** – If a serving member is feeling stalemated in the military, not getting opportunities for deployment, doing work that is not personally meaningful, feeling unrecognized, or just not fitting in to the military structure, they may opt out, believing that they can better manage their careers within the civilian world.

Members who have left the CAF may experience a loss of identity. They may miss the authority they exercised or the discipline of the military environment. The Armed Forces provided a goal-oriented, driven, and structured lifestyle—a 24/7 occupation in or out of uniform.[20] While serving, members had few opportunities to completely disengage from the military lifestyle. They wore a uniform that denoted their standing and their commitment to their country. They experienced challenges and adventures found in few other work environments. When a member leaves the military, they leave all of this behind. It can feel like losing a part of themselves—who they are as a person.

Figure 2 depicts the many places the life of a service member may intersect with military culture. The more overlapping intersection points and the more intense the intersected experiences, the more difficult the transition is likely to be. But due to the immersive nature of military culture, one's role, class, profession, spirituality, gender, age, and family identity can become undifferentiated from or subsumed under the larger military cultural identity. Factoring in how many aspects of the military member's identity are connected with the military culture and lifestyle may help us better understand and assist those who are struggling with the losses associated with leaving and the creation of a new purpose.

Figure 2: Overlapping Identities

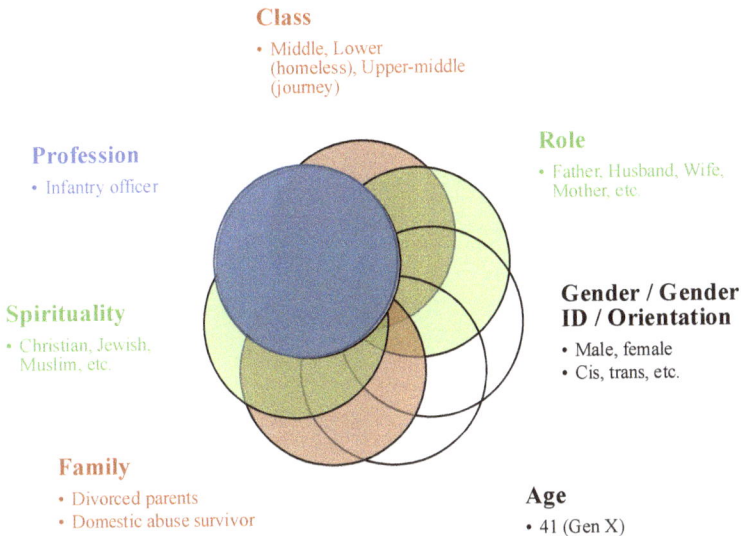

Class
- Middle, Lower (homeless), Upper-middle (journey)

Profession
- Infantry officer

Role
- Father, Husband, Wife, Mother, etc.

Gender / Gender ID / Orientation
- Male, female
- Cis, trans, etc.

Spirituality
- Christian, Jewish, Muslim, etc.

Family
- Divorced parents
- Domestic abuse survivor

Age
- 41 (Gen X)

Source: Jordan Camarda, "Military Cultural Competence," presentation at Cannexus 2024

In other words, the longer a member was in the Forces or the more intense their experiences, the longer the adjustment period might be. Veterans have to come to terms with life in the civilian world and, if necessary, take time to grieve the things they miss about military life and the identity it provided. Veterans also have to adjust to things heretofore provided by the military, such as access to military rental housing, employment, health care, and income. They may have to retrain for a different job or go back to school, adjust to a civilian work culture, and more.

The loss of identity is huge for some. We need to know that and be prepared to help them carve out a new cultural identity in the civilian world—one that is meaningful and purpose driven.

Some Noteworthy Statistics

What do Veterans need in addition to a new identity? The following numbers help us to understand areas of need, which is key to helping.

- A 2020 qualitative study by Veterans Affairs Canada[21] of 80 CAF members and Veterans (91% Regular Force and 9% Reserve Force) it was found that while some had successfully transitioned to new careers, others were experiencing difficulties getting hired, limited opportunities to work, and their military skills not translating well to civilian roles. Many also struggled with the impact of being out of uniform and the loss of identity that resulted.

- In the 2019 Life After Service Studies (LASS) survey,[22] 45% of Regular Force Veterans reported a fairly easy adjustment to civilian life while 39% found it difficult. Officers reported the lowest difficulty rate (21%). Junior non-commissioned members (47%) had the most adjustment challenges, rating it as very or moderately difficult.

- Census data (2021) show that 97,625 Canadians served in the Canadian Armed Forces (CAF), with 461,240 Veterans, the first such profile in 50 years.[23] Almost a third of these Veterans are in the core working age of 25–54.

- Spouses/partners of Veterans are significantly affected by their release with 32% experiencing challenges along with 23% of their children.[24]

- A 2022 National Veteran Employment Strategy consultation with 1,016 participants (945 in English and 71 in French) revealed concerns about insufficient transition time, frustrations in translating military experience to civilian roles, and age biases in finding work.[25]

- Pre-release income for women was $64,490 compared to $71,710 for men, with post-release income declining by 19% for women and only 0.2% for men.[26]

- Almost 25% of recently released Veterans were not in the labour force, with many reporting barriers like stigma and difficulty translating military experience.[27]

Supports/Networks and Outreach

A core component of military culture is teamwork. Consequently, serving military members, Veterans, and their families benefit most when they have a support network—connections to people who speak their language, understand what they've been through, and can provide training, mentorship, employment, links to employers, and information about available support services. The greater the extent to which family members, career practitioners, professional associations, service providers as well as Veterans collaborate in sharing knowledge, resources, and best practices, the fewer former service personnel will be neglected.

Education and Training

If one entered the CAF with only a Grade 10 education and worked in a military occupation that has no direct civilian equivalent, it is more than likely that some degree of further education or retraining will be needed on leaving military service to meet established civilian education requirements for employment. However, there is also a significant probability that service personnel in these occupations possess skills and experiences desirable across a broad range of careers, particularly if they served in more senior roles. Now that transitioning members are allocated time to connect with CAF TG prior to leaving, it will help to facilitate their readiness for civilian life.[28]

Then there is the credentialism issue. How do service members with military credentials and training leverage them in civilian life? Do institutions provide credit for military training, courses, or work experience? If yes, which ones? What documentation is required? How do we easily disseminate this information to Veterans? We will look at some answers to these questions in Chapter 8.

Side note: As an institution, the CAF recognizes and supports academic advancement. There are many pathways available within the CAF for members to upgrade their credentials, and at most promotion boards, academic achievements equate to additional points towards promotion. Similarly, VAC directly supports and promotes Veterans in upgrading their education through the **Education and Training Benefit** (https://www.veterans.gc.ca/en/education-and-jobs/go-back-school/education-and-training-benefit), which offers funding to Veterans to pursue the education they desire.

Employment

In the 2019 Life After Service Studies (LASS) survey, 60% of Regular Force Veterans were employed, with senior non-commissioned members having the lowest employment rate at 50% (these members are likely older at the time of transition and possessed only a high school education at the time of joining), compared to officers at 58% and junior non-commissioned members at 66%.[29] Furthermore, 52% of Veterans were working in jobs that utilized their military skills and knowledge, and close to 75% of those who

---

had worked since their release reported that the experiences, education, and training received during service helped them to secure their current or most recent civilian employment.[30]

While the labour market outcomes for CAF Veterans are, on average, fairly positive, subgroups are experiencing challenges. Part II of this guide will cover the topic of employment in more detail, but here are some of the key employment-related needs:

- Job-finding information
- Tools and resources specific to Veterans
- Addressing employer myths/fears about hiring Veterans or those returning from a tour of duty who might be called up again
- Translating military experience into civilian workplace language
- Information on civilian-to-military job equivalencies
- Overcoming obstacles to employment (under-education, financial, disabilities)
- Creating civilian resumes, understanding labour market information, and preparing for civilian job interviews
- Dealing with work-culture transition, e.g., moving from hierarchy and conformity to being your own career manager
- Accessing jobs and military-friendly employers
- Income drops upon transition

In an interview with Elaine Piper, a now-retired career development consultant who developed and also taught a course for career practitioners on working with military clientele,[31] she noted the following needs and challenges expressed by transitioning members:

- Career decision-making. Some transitioning members or Veterans don't know what they want and think "any job" will do. They need help in knowing themselves and thinking differently about what they have to offer.

- Not enough access and connections to industry professional associations that can provide them with the lingo, acknowledgement, network, and training they may need, and help them translate what they've done into civilian terminology and civilian industry certifications.

- Some feel they don't have a purpose now that they have left the military and need assistance in creating a new purpose, post-service.

- Dealing with biases in the community and with employers/recruiters.

- Knowing what is appropriate and not appropriate to share with employers about life in the CAF.

- Lack of savvy with social media tools.

- Asking for help. Some find it hard to ask for help and hard to say, "I am struggling."

- Navigating what might be a different mindset in the civilian work world.

    o In the military, mission, service, and team are the focus. In the civilian context, it's typically individual, family, community. Thinking of self first is hard.

    o In the military, one does not leave until the mission is complete. So when a civilian colleague checks out at 5 pm with a task left incomplete, those two mindsets may clash.

- Negotiating for yourself and justifying why you've earned a raise or promotion. This is very different from the military where likely one is recommended for that promotion based on outstanding work. Teaching Veterans how to track and document their accomplishments is critical.

Leaving Because of Illness or Injury

Imagine the plight of the soldier who has not chosen to leave the CAF but must. He has been injured. He knows the drill. A member of the CAF must be ready to perform a broad range of tasks, not just the duties of his specific occupation. The fact that he can no longer meet this universality of service principle means he can no longer wear the uniform.[32] Leaving is hard enough, especially if that identity meant a lot to him. Now, on top of that loss this Veteran has to deal with the losses associated with the injury itself. How will this affect his work and life on a daily basis?

Approximately 20% of Canadian Veterans experience depression, PTSD, and anxiety disorders. Among those with a diagnosed mental health challenge, 95% report a physical health issue.[33] Career practitioners can be that much more helpful to ill or injured Veterans if we have at least a rudimentary knowledge of these conditions and the resources available to support those who have them. More importantly, as part of our counselling process, we must remember to ascertain if our client is mentally, physically, emotionally, and spiritually ready to look for work. Sometimes there are more pressing needs that must be met first. And even when the financial need for employment is as important as these other needs, we must still ensure that our clients are stabilized or are receiving supports before they embark on their employment quest.

Support Networks for At-risk Transitioning Members/Veterans

We have already established that connecting to peer networks is a key component in helping Veterans adapt to life after military service. Below are a few of the services, including the National Resource Directory, available to help Veterans cope with injuries and/or illnesses acquired during service.

Canadian Armed Forces Transition Group

(https://www.canada.ca/en/department-national-defence/corporate/reports-publications/transition-guide/about-the-caf-transition-group.html) offers a range of supports for ill and injured members including:

- **The Digital Transition Centre**. This includes virtual access to transition counselling, electronic release administration, access to transition training and education initiatives, and access to the National Resource Directory.

- The **National Resource Directory** houses military, Veteran, and family supportive organizations across all domains of well-being and sectors in Canadian society.

- **Return to Duty Program** (RTD). Ill and injured members are offered professional supports across all domains of well-being as they heal and explore alternative career pathways within the military.

- **Vocational Rehabilitation for Serving Members** (VRPSM). During the last six months of their service, members who are transitioning out of the military for medical reasons are able to test out working in the civilian sphere and find that path that's best for them.

- **Soldier On**. This program provides opportunities and resources through recreation and creative activities and is recognized for improving the quality of life of ill and injured members and Veterans.

Operational Stress Injury and Social Support (OSISS)

https://cfmws.ca/support-services/health-wellness/mental-health/operational-stress-injury-social-support-(osiss)

OSISS, a partnership between CAF and Veterans Affairs Canada, provides peer-to-peer support to CAF members, Veterans or families of former CAF members dealing with the impact of operational stress injuries (OSIs). An OSI is defined as any persistent psychological difficulty that is a result of operational duties while in military service. OSIs include post-traumatic stress disorder (PTSD), anxiety, depression, or any condition that impacts one's ability to function in daily tasks. Since its inception, OSISS has created a nationwide Peer Support Network that offers a listening ear and referrals as needed.

Wounded Warriors Canada

https://woundedwarriors.ca/

Wounded Warriors is a national mental health service committed to helping individuals, family members, and organizations living with or exposed to trauma. Working in conjunction with mental health service organizations, they provide culturally informed programs, using counselling, education, and training tools to support clients in developing resiliency and recovering from trauma. Programs include trauma resiliency for warriors, couples resiliency, warrior kids camps, and surviving family workshops. Funding, support, training, and pairing of service dogs is also part of their operations.

Veterans Transition Network

https://www.vtncanada.org

Using research-backed programs, Veterans Transition Network helps CAF and RCMP members and Veterans overcome difficulties transitioning out of service and the psychological impact. Transition courses are offered at two levels. Level 1 is a five-day in-person retreat that aims to empower Veterans and normalize their transition journey. Key elements of this course include communication skills, personal development, self-maintenance, future planning, and social engagement. Level 2 is a five-day in-person retreat featuring intensive therapy that helps clients repair their sense of self, rebuild their ability to trust, and restore their values using enactment scenarios.

VETS Canada (Veterans Emergency Transition Services)

https://vetscanada.org

VETS was launched in 2010–2011, when Veteran Jim Lowther realized that many fellow Veterans had not made successful transitions to civilian life. Some had lost their families, were suicidal, homeless, unemployed or struggling to cope with mental or physical illnesses. Now, VETS is a federally registered non-profit charity with over 1,440 volunteers across Canada that not only helps homeless Veterans but those experiencing difficulty of any kind like paying a bill, buying groceries or facing a mental health crisis. The service has helped over 4,500 Veterans to date.

Veterans Affairs Canada

https://www.veterans.gc.ca/en/services

Several complementary peer support and stand-alone programs are available to help Veterans and their families. Some of these include:

- **Support for Operational Stress Injury (SOSI)** https://www.veterans.gc.ca/en/mental-and-physical-health/mental-health-and-wellness/counselling-services/talk-someone-who-can-relate: This is a national peer support network for Veterans and current members of the Royal Canadian Mounted Police (RCMP) dealing with daily life challenges due to their service.

- **Family Peer Support Coordinators** https://www.veterans.gc.ca/en/families-and-caregivers/health-programs-and-services/support-families-and-caregivers: These coordinators offer support to families dealing with the effects of operational stress injuries, helping them navigate the challenges and providing a community of understanding.

- **Military Sexual Trauma Peer Support Program** https://www.canada.ca/en/department-national-defence/services/benefits-military/health-support/sexual-misconduct-response/peer-support-program.html: In partnership with the Department of National Defence, this program offers trauma-informed peer support services for those affected by sexual misconduct or military sexual trauma during their service.

- **Atlas Institute for Veterans and Families** https://atlasveterans.ca/knowledge-hub/peer-support/: This institute provides an interactive directory and map to find peer support programs and services available to Veterans and their families across Canada.

- **Case Management** https://www.veterans.gc.ca/en/mental-and-physical-health/case-management: Provides personalized support for Veterans facing complex challenges. Case managers work directly with Veterans to identify their needs, set goals, and create a plan to help them achieve their highest level of independence, health, and well-being.

- **Veterans Independence Program (VIP)** https://www.veterans.gc.ca/en/about-vac/reports-policies-and-legislation/departmental-reports/privacy-impact-assessment-pia/veterans-independence-program: Provides services such as grounds maintenance, housekeeping, meal delivery, and professional healthcare support to help Veterans maintain their independence.

- **Veterans Homelessness Program (VHP)** https://www.veterans.gc.ca/en/housing-and-home-life/risk-housing-situation/understanding-veteran-homelessness/veterans-homelessness-support: Offers rent supplements, mental health support, and financial assistance to help Veterans transition into stable homes.

- **Assistance Service 24-hour Toll-free Line** https://www.veterans.gc.ca/en/mental-and-physical-health/mental-health-and-wellness/counselling-services/talk-mental-health-professional: The Canadian Armed Forces Member Assistance Program and Veterans Affairs Canada Assistance Service offer 24/7 support through a toll-free line at **1-800-268-7708** or **1-800-567-5803** (TDD). This service for Canadian Armed Forces members, Military, and Royal Canadian Mounted Police Veterans, ensures immediate access to assistance whenever needed.

Remember that different Veterans have different needs! Remember too to collaborate, where possible, with other career practitioners to share and gain knowledge.

* * *

So there you have it—a look at the needs and challenges! Those most directly related to helping CAF Veterans in their journey from military to civilian employment will be the focus of the rest of this guide, starting with a refresher on transition theories and approaches.

★ Career practitioners should address readiness for employment as well as the losses experienced by Veterans when they leave military service.

★ Access to networks and resources to assist in finding employment is critical to Veterans seeking civilian employment.

★ Veterans may present with different mindsets that career professionals must seek to understand.

★ A vast network of services and resources are available to support ill and/or injured members and Veterans.

★ Career practitioners can help with creating a new purpose.

CHAPTER 4

Understanding Transition

The Canadian Armed Forces Transition Group (CAF TG) has shifted its focus from a culture of release to a culture of transition. It defines transition as a "period of re-integration from military to life after service and the corresponding process of change that a serving member, Veteran or their family go through when their service is completed."[34] "Reintegration" and "process of change" are the key elements emphasized. CAF TG also takes the position that because what happens during transition affects the entire support network of the transitioning member, that entire network should be factored into transitioning plans. Seamless and integrated, it aims to deliver personalized, professional and standardized supports to military members and their families.

While the transition process may begin in the Canadian Armed Forces Transition Group, Veterans Affairs Canada is engaged early on in the process and throughout the transition journey. As the member and their family formally release from the Canadian Armed Forces, Veterans Affairs Canada continues that support throughout their post-service life. As civilian career practitioners, it is vital to be aware that both the CAF and VAC support the member and their families throughout the process.

Transition services have come a long way since the first edition of this guide was published. CAF members can now establish their transition goals along seven **Domains of Well-Being**—interconnected areas of a Veteran's life that need to be supported during and after their transition (Fig. 3).[35] The domains are as follows:

1. Purpose – planning for activities one finds beneficial and meaningful

2. Finances – what to do to achieve financial security

3. Social Integration – how to maintain supportive relationships and community engagement

4. Life Skills – what is needed to adapt to and cope with civilian life

5. Housing and Physical Environment – securing safe, adequate, and affordable housing

6. Cultural and Social Environment – the need to be understood, valued, and appreciated

7. Health – what is needed to function well physically, mentally, socially, and spiritually

Figure 3: Domains of Well-Being

MILITARY 2 CIVILIAN EMPLOYMENT

The CAF TG offers transitioning support to military members throughout their military career but most intensively in the six months prior to leaving service. The last 30 days of that six-month period is considered a "protected period" where activities associated with the member's transition plan are prioritized over other work tasks.[36] Whether in person at one of 27 Transition Centres across Canada, or online via the Digital Transition Centre (https://military-transition.canada.ca/en/), members can access a comprehensive Transition Guide, live transition counselling, transition training, and access to the National Resource Directory of trusted organizations that offer support to the military, Veteran, and family communities.

CAF TG initiates the transition process and then hands off to Veterans Affairs Canada for post-release support, particularly for those medically releasing and requiring case management.

But CAF TG and VAC cannot do it all. Services provided by career development professionals like you and me are also part of the transition resources our vets can utilize. And to do that well, a review of relevant transition theories and approaches might help those of us who could use a refresher be more robustly equipped to be of service to those going through the military-to-civilian transition.

Transitioning: Approaches and Strategies

Clients seeking our professional assistance are not always clear about what they want from us or what they want us to do for them. We can help them by providing information to increase their self-knowledge, information about career options, guidance in decision-making, and assessment of their career readiness.

Do not hesitate to ask a client why they've come to seek your services. What do they hope you can do for them? Why now? What prompted them to book an appointment? Asking questions like these allows us to hear and determine if we are the appropriate "solution" for their need. Sometimes we're not.

Many are the models that try to capture the elements involved in life transitions and most transition formulations can be summarized in three stages: understanding transition, negotiating transition, and resolving transition.[37] Let's take a look at five approaches and strategies that can be both effective and relevant in helping our Veteran clients as they seek to understand, negotiate, and resolve the process of their own military-to-civilian transition.

[Note: While our primary focus is on helping our clients in their career development, sometimes it becomes obvious that other personal issues need to be addressed before the client can continue with their career plans. Practitioners who do not have professional training in therapeutic interventions should tactfully discuss this with the client and offer, if needed, referral to an appropriate professional].

Transition Planning — Schlossberg's 4-S Model

Faced with the pressing need to find a job or get an education, the "new" Veteran may not take time—or see the need to take time—to come to terms with the past before launching into the future. However, *events* (like leaving the CAF) and *non-events* (the expectation of something that never materializes) are both life-changing. Changes are transitions. This is why Mary Anderson and Jane Goodman recommend Schlossberg's 4-S Model for working with Veterans as they move through the transition process.[38]

This model, which focuses on Situation, Self, Support, and Strategies, can help practitioners plan interventions in line with the client's strengths and liabilities, to enhance their coping and adaptation, especially as they move from a work system that was hierarchical and conforming to one that is more focused on self-reliance and self-promotion. The model will also connect with serving military members and Veterans as it mirrors some of the core elements they are taught to plan and execute missions.

The model provides questions for each area of focus;

- The **Situation** question—"What is happening now?"—give the transitioning member a chance to take stock. Answers can vary widely: "I'm leaving the military after ___ [number of] years," "I am injured," "My family dynamics have changed," "I am not sure what job I can get."

- The **Self** question—"How am I perceiving myself during this transition?"—can also be framed as "How am I really doing?" This allows the client to examine his or her feelings. Fear? Excitement? Anxiety? Our personal and psychological resources—values, spirituality, resilience, and life outlook—come into play every time we are challenged by changes.

- **Support** is so important as people make life transitions. This is particularly apropos for transitioning military members. They need the support of family, friends, networks, employers, career professionals and peers. They need a space or place to speak honestly and receive affirmation, feedback and assistance. Key questions are "What supports do I have?" and "What supports do I need?"

- **Strategies**: "How do I typically cope with change?" "What mechanisms do I use to help me prepare for the unexpected?" Coping strategies help us to control the impact or meaning of a problem, modify the situation and manage stress. Individuals cope best when they are flexible and are prepared to employ more than one strategy.

For those who prefer a more simplified approach, Schlossberg's model can be reframed in the form of these four questions for your client to ponder:

- What is happening now? (Situation)
- How am I doing? (Self)
- What do I need? (Support)
- How do I cope? (Strategies)

Cognitive Information Processing (CIP)

Cognitive Information Processing is a set of theoretical perspectives dealing with how we sequence and execute cognitive events. It focuses on what happens between input (receiving information) and output (executing the information). As illustrated in Figure 4, CIP theory purports that all career problem-solving and decision-making involves a pyramid of knowledge (self and of occupational), decision-making skills, and metacognitions.

Figure 4: CIP Theory

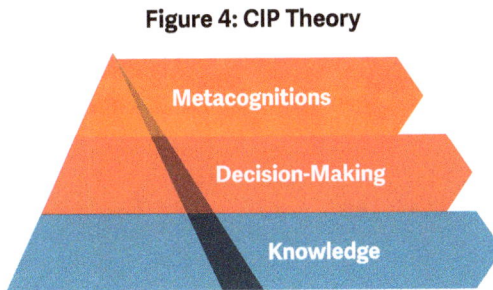

Metacognitions

Decision-Making

Knowledge

Level 1: Knowledge Domain
(knowing about myself, knowing about my options)

Self-knowledge: At the base of the pyramid, this step includes information about a client's employment interests, skills, values, aptitudes, and personality attributes. These can be obtained from card sorts, inventories, worksheets, or online resources like the Self-Directed Search®(SDS).

Occupational Knowledge: Accompanying self-knowledge is occupational information: Researching employers, person-to-person, or online networking, employment websites, military-to-civilian skills translators, informational interviews, career and employment fairs.

Level 2: Decision-Making Skills Domain
(knowing how I make decisions)

Communication, Analysis, Synthesis, Valuing, and Execution (CASVE), a five-phase decision-making model, can help the Veteran client determine the best first step and also steps toward longer-term goals. In layperson's terms, CASVE can be reframed by asking the following questions:

- Communication – What is the gap? What is the issue that needs my attention?

- Analysis – What are the components of the issue(s)?

- Synthesis – What are my alternatives?

- Valuing – Which options are priority?

- Execution – What am I going to do to get to the outcomes I want?

The authors of the CASVE model suggest this sequence for delivering career interventions[39]:

- Step 1 – Conduct initial interview with client.

- Step 2 – Do a preliminary assessment to determine client's readiness.

- Step 3 – Work with client to define the career problem(s) and analyze causes.

- Step 4 – Collaborate with client to formulate achievable problem-solving and decision-making goals.

- Step 5 – Provide client with a list of activities and resources they need (individual learning plans).

- Step 6 – Require client to execute their individual learning plans.

- Step 7 – Conduct a summative review of client's progress and generalize new learning to other career problems.

Level 3: Metacognitions Domain
(thinking about my decision making)

At this stage, clients analyze (executive processing) the decisions they have made. They ask, "How am I feeling about this decision?" By probing for any negative thoughts the client has that might impact the job-search process, career practitioners can challenge the negative thoughts and work with the client to alter negative self-messages. Examples of negative thoughts are "I'm not good enough," "No one will hire me because of my disability," and so on.

The authors of CIP have also developed the Career Thoughts Inventory (CTI) which helps to measure "dysfunctional thinking" in the career decision-making process such as anxiety about making a career commitment, confusion or external conflicts. Accompanying the CTI is the Career Thoughts Inventory Workbook. It helps clients in reframing the negative thoughts identified. This is also where developing individualized learning plans can ensure clients have tangible tools and strategies to keep them on track moving forward.

Mary Buzzetta et al. make the case that CIP can also be used to help transitioning military personnel who are facing real or imagined career or employment barriers.[40] For example, moving from a highly structured and team-oriented work environment to a civilian workplace that is less structured and individual-oriented can be construed as a barrier, generating negative self-talk like, "I'll never learn to function in a place where the rules are always changing." There is also the loss of identity the released member experiences—loss of role and status.

By exploring the client's career thoughts and applying the CASVE model, career practitioners can help clients begin to identify potential areas of challenge and refer out as needed. The National Resource Directory is recommended here as well.

Solution-Focused Coaching[41]

"What if whatever problem you're experiencing right now got fixed—what would your life look like?" Coaches using the Solution-Focused Therapy approach ask this type of question.[42] No longer restricted to the realm of psychotherapy, solution-focused coaching operates on two key premises: (1) individualized and personalized coaching solutions work best, and (2) people each have the ability to solve their own problem. It is respectful, collaborative and brief. (I've included this approach more for information than for practice—unless one is certified in Solution-Focused Coaching or Therapy). Here are the steps clients will walk through:

1. Acknowledge the problem. How is this a problem? How does it affect me?

2. Define the difference you want to achieve. How would my future look if this were not a problem?

3. Identify what will help you achieve the outcome you desire.

4. Focus on doing more of what works and less of what doesn't.

The Veteran who cannot find work and is mired in negativity or hopelessness, the client who has little patience for a drawn out process-oriented counselling strategy, or the individual having difficulty articulating how her military career has equipped her with skills employers want—all can benefit from a solution-focused coaching approach. Refer your client to the appropriate service provider if this is not an area you are skilled in.

Strength-Based Coaching/Counselling

Often clients solicit the assistance of career professionals to help them find a particular job without first determining if the job is a good fit. Helping the client assess the strengths they possess and learn how to articulate these to a prospective employer can be very liberating. Strengths can come in the form of personality attributes, competencies, aptitudes or skills. Ask:

- When are you at your best?

- Describe a peak moment in your life.

- What gives you energy and makes you feel good about yourself?

- Tell me about three good things in your life?

The above questions are meant to draw out a person's inherent and energizing capacities. *Energizing* is the operative word in this approach. Infused with elements of positive psychology, strength-based coaching focuses not on the things clients do poorly, but on helping them become better at the things they do well.[43]

Watch what happens when you ask a client to talk about a peak moment or engagement in an activity that uses their best skills. Her face lights up. His eyes shine. She sounds articulate and confident. They sound excited.

Now see the difference when you ask that same person to talk about their weaknesses. The posture droops. The energy drops. The sun sets.

As with the solution-focused approach, strength-based coaching/counselling can be an excellent model to use with Veterans looking for work.

Legacy Careers® Approach[44]

Retirement from military service can occur at a traditional retirement age or at a relatively young age. Whether younger or older, the Veteran who has amassed skills, experiences, relationships and knowledge, and wants to focus future efforts on addressing challenges and opportunities that matter to them can benefit from the Legacy Careers® Approach. It involves:

- Taking stock
- Identifying meaning
- Creating a plan
- Leaving a legacy

This approach does not focus on translating military experience to fit a civilian job posting. Rather, it is concerned with providing tools and strategies to help the Veteran establish an identity in civilian life that is meaningful and forward-looking. The Legacy Careers® Approach acknowledges that there is a broad spectrum of possibilities, from continuing to do the same type of work to not finding new paid work at all. It prompts the Veteran to ask: "What do I want to use the next phase of my life to do?"

For the career practitioner, rather than starting with the Knowledge Domain outlined in Level 1 of the CIP Approach (self-assessment and career options), we can help focus the client on the essential criteria that must be met to ensure they feel secure and satisfied in their next career. The following self-reflection questions can help the Veteran with this process:

- What do I need and want?

- What do I care about?

- What are my innate talents (as opposed to learned skills)?

- What impact should my work have? What problems do I want to be part of solving?

The Legacy Careers® Approach does not assume that people will continue on a linear career path, remain in the same industry or maintain the same level or rank they had in their previous career. Instead, it allows them to take a step back from titles, roles, and specific job duties to identify what meaning they want their work to have and what steps they need to take to move from where they are now to where they want to be. Often, the process involves retraining, internships, temporary jobs or a multi-step plan.

The Legacy Careers® Approach identifies what clients will be doing over the next six months, 1–2 years and 5–10 years to continually grow and evolve into their full "Legacy Career." By taking a 10- to 20-year horizon, practitioners can work with transitioning military clients to build a plan that

- meets their short- and long-term needs,

- focuses on their innate talents (as opposed to areas where they have acquired skills),

- involves work that they care about, and

- makes an impact that is recognized in today's market.

Military members and Veterans exploring career transition can use the Careers SweetSpot tool (https://community.challengefactory.ca/find-your-career-sweetspot/) to first identify the criteria they would like their Legacy Career to meet, and then assess real potential roles against those criteria.

* * *

The above approaches are by no means the only options. You might prefer to use your own trusted and proven techniques when working with clients going through life transitions. Because career practitioners are not psychotherapists, we know our limits but are still able to recognize when clients' "dysfunction-al cognitions" go beyond the scope of our expertise. The MTEP National Resource Directory (https://military-transition.canada.ca/en/national-re-source-directory) is an important tool to help us and our clients identify and access a comprehensive range of supports that meet their mental health needs.

★ Transitions involves understanding, negotiating and resolving.

★ Different approaches can be customized or combined to meet our clients' needs.

★ A new sense of purpose can be created using elements of transition approaches.

YVONNE'S FAVOURITES

◎ *The Canadian Guide to Hiring Veterans* can help identify employers who are Veteran friendly.

◎ The Domains of Well-Being diagram (https://www.canada.ca/en/department-national-defence/services/benefits-military/transition/mtep.html) that identifies the range of life areas impacted during transitions.

"The family has been an incredible frame against which I've been able to do the things that I have."

—Deputy Commander (Air Force) (Retired)

CHAPTER 5

Becoming Military Cultural Competent

If and when a military member or Veteran reaches out to us, it is extremely important that we not only understand the value they bring to the workplace but are equipped with the competencies required to better serve this population of clients. They need to know that we "get" them. Honouring the military cultural identity of serving members, Veterans, and families is essential in building a solid foundation of trust.

According to Hazel Atuel and Carl Castro,[45] the military as an organization is different from other groups. It has its own social and cultural norms, values, and expectations. Therefore, the better our understanding of that culture and the more aware we are of our attitudes, cognitions, and biases with respect to those who serve in the military, the more effective we will be as service providers.

Our beliefs are value-laden. Positive beliefs will likely foster positive therapeutic rapport, and negative beliefs—the opposite. Regardless of our position on warfare, our primary responsibility is to serve our clients well. Part of that means owning that we may have biases and, having identified them, being prepared to put them aside or refer elsewhere if we cannot do so.

So let's get some background information before delving into what constitutes military cultural competent counselling.

Major (Retired) Jordan Camarda currently leads as National Manager for the Military Transition Engagement and Partnership team. One of his core responsibilities is that of educating service providers on the competencies needed to effectively engage with and best support transitioning military members and Veterans. I attended a presentation he offered at Cannexus 2024 (CERIC's annual career development conference) and have *carte blanche* permission to share his content with you.

Of the 97,625 members currently serving in the Canadian Armed Forces, 20% are women, 3.5% are Indigenous people, and 11.8% are visible minorities.[46] These members can be found serving across Canada in urban, rural, and isolated locations within the Army, Navy, Air Force, and Special Operations. We also know from data derived from the 2021 Census that veterans within the 25–64 age group represents a potential workforce of 259,605 people, many of whom could benefit from the career and employment counselling/coaching we provide.[47]

Many Veterans struggle with a loss of identity once they leave service. The team connectedness, the shared mission and purpose, knowing where you stand in the chain of command—these are all losses that may contribute to a loss of self. That loss however is not unique to Veterans. I personally recall an incident on a trip to the United States after I had just left a role that I had held for many years. The border official asked me what my occupation was. It threw me. I was no longer what I was, and not yet what I was to become. In that limbo space lies a quagmire of uncertainty that the assistance of an understanding and astute career practitioner can help to traverse.

Five Steps to Military Cultural Competence

Camarda offers a roadmap to military cultural competence made up of five steps (Fig. 5).

Figure 5: A Roadmap to Military Cultural Competence

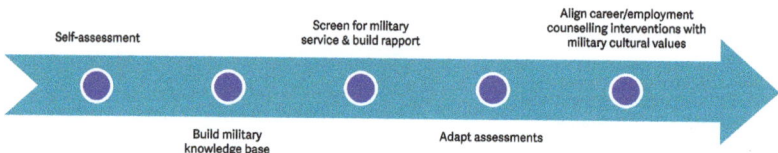

Self-assessment

Screen for military service & build rapport

Align career/employment counselling interventions with military cultural values

Build military knowledge base

Adapt assessments

Source: Jordan Camarda, "Military Cultural Competence," presentation at Cannexus 2024

Step 1 – Self-assessment

As counsellors, we need to adopt a spirit of "cultural humility and curiosity."[48] We should invite the client to tell us about their life in service (as much as they are able to share) without bias, judgement, or prejudice on our part. An attitude of "I am really curious and interested to understand you. Please tell me more," puts the client in the position of teacher. How empowering! This step also includes assessing if our beliefs and attitudes show that we value or devalue the military or Veteran client. The Centre for Deployment Psychology offers a useful self-awareness exercise that we can complete to determine our views/biases,[49] as well as a checklist to help us build military cultural competencies.[50] The exercise invites us to consider our beliefs about people who are comfortable around firearms, our views about people who have taken a life, our views on what it means to serve and the types of people who join the military, and a range of statements that we do not regularly think about.

Step 2 – Build a Military Knowledge Base

In addition to allowing ourselves to be educated by our client, we must also take the initiative to read and discover on our own. What do I need to know about the life this client comes from to help them most effectively? The fact that you are reading this guide and have gotten this far demonstrates that curiosity that so energizes our work. (See Chapter 12 for a few other knowledge-building links.) And when the Veteran client begins to work with us, it means we offer them the courtesy of acknowledging their title and rank. This can be one way of honouring their military cultural identity.

Step 3 – Screen for Military Service and Build Rapport

Camarda recommends that in our intake processes—whether forms, interviews, or both—we include a question about CAF service. If that is checked by our client, we can then ask about what element they served in (Army, Navy, Air Force, Special Forces), their rank, years of service, and whether or not they were deployed. (Do not ask them to provide deployment details on the form. This is more of an in-person conversation and you have to be attuned to whether or not the client wants to talk about it.) "What was your occupation in the military?" is a key question that can build rapport. Trust comes when you show genuine interest in what they did. A question like "What were your most satisfying moments as an Infantry Officer?" can open doors of trust and is a way of again honouring their military identity. In asking these questions we will be better equipped to have "culturally informed interactions," says Camarda.

Step 4 – Adapt Assessments

We can adapt our assessments to address early critical information about our clients, like why are they transitioning out of the military and their readiness for change. (Note: The Mental Health Continuum Model is a noteworthy tool the CAF uses in its Road to Mental Readiness training and education program.[51] If your client is exhibiting any of the behaviours in the danger zones [orange and red], a referral to mental health service providers may be in order.)

Reasons for leaving military service fall into one of four categories: end of service, medical, voluntary, or unsuitability. If our Veteran client is stuck in the life left behind, caught between competing priorities like wanting to return to service versus staying with family, angry about being released, or trying to find traction in the civilian world, we can factor these in our strategies. Asking the right questions will also help us understand where there might be resistance. Readiness is the key— for both the Veteran and us.

Atuel and Carl identify three common affective, behavioural, and cognitive paradoxes transitioning military clients or Veterans may present:[52]

- **Courage Paradox:** Having honed how to be strong and courageous in the face of battle, clients often view asking for help as weakness—especially if they are experiencing difficulty or feeling emotional.

- **Back-there Paradox:** This is where the Veteran client is caught between two equally important families—their service family and their civilian family. The client wants to be with both at the same time.

- **Modesty Paradox:** In this instance, the client feels that they should receive recognition for the sacrifices and service they have made **and** grapples with the fact that many civilians do not care or are not even open to helping Veterans.

It bears repeating: Gauging where the military client is and using assessment tools that speak their language will help build rapport, trust, and comfort.

Step 5 – Align Career/Employment Counselling Interventions with Military Cultural Values

This is where we ensure our career and employment approach is sensitive to the formerly held rank and seniority level of the member seeking our services. Tables 2 and 3* help us understand the scope of responsibility for both commissioned officers and non-commissioned members along with the approximate civilian equivalents. Bear in mind as you review the table that while rank provides a general guide to one's position in the CAF, Camarda notes that it is the combination of rank, occupation, unit, position, and experiences that provides the most accurate picture of what a client did in the military. For example, some Captains may have more strategic experience than some Colonels.

Table 2: Commissioned Officer (CO) Ranks and Their Civilian Equivalents

Military rank	Civilian equivalent	Level and scope of responsibility
• General • Admiral	• Senior Executive • CEO • Senior Advisor	• Develops policies and institutional processes • Has extensive and high-level leadership expertise • Oversees extremely large organizational portfolios in excess of 10,000 staff
• Commander • Colonel • Captain (N)	• Executive • Managing Director	• Strategic planning and policy development • Has extensive leadership experience • Oversees large-scale resource management for 5,000+ staff
• Lieutenant-Colonel Commander • Major Lieutenant-Commander	• Middle/Senior Manager • Branch Manager	• Provides senior mentorship, develops policy, manages resources • More hands-on leadership and management of projects • Responsible for 100–1,500 staff
• Captain • Lieutenant (N) • Lieutenant Sub-Lieutenant	• Junior/Assistant Manager • Team Leader	• Expert trainer or instructor • Provides leadership development and resource management for 10–50 staff
• Second Lieutenant • Acting Sub-Lieutenant(N) • Officer Cadet	• Individual Contributor/ Team Member	• Trainee learning and developing in occupational area and earning qualifications or education

Supplied by Dwayne L. Cormier and Jordan Camarda, CAF TG. (Updated rank information can be sourced at https://www.canada.ca/en/services/defence/caf/military-identity-system/rank-appointment-insignia.html.)

Table 3: Non-Commissioned Member (NCM) Ranks and Their Civilian Equivalents

Military rank	Civilian equivalent	Level and scope of responsibility
• Chief Warrant Officer • Chief Petty Officer 1st Class • Master Warrant Officer • Chief Petty Officer 2nd Class	• Middle- or senior-level manager • Senior supervisor, advisor, trainer	• Highly qualified with extensive leadership experience • Responsible for 100+ staff
• Warrant Officer • Petty Officer 1st Class • Sergeant • Petty Officer 2nd Class	• Foreperson, middle or junior manager/supervisor • Trainer/ Instructor	• Hands-on technical leader experienced in resource management • Responsible for 30–100 staff
• Master Corporal • Master Sailor	• Small-team leader with expertise in a particular occupation or trade	• Provides junior leadership training or instruction • Has basic management skills • Responsible for 5–30 staff
• Corporal • Sailor, 1st Class	• Expert worker in a particular occupation or trade area • A team member	• Has some leadership, training, and instructional skills • Is developing skills and working toward occupational certification
• Private • Sailor, 3rd Class • Aviator	• Individual contributor and team member	• Is in training and development • Is acquiring certification and educational credentials

Supplied by Dwayne L. Cormier and Jordan Camarda, CAF TG. (Updated rank information can be sourced at https://www.canada.ca/en/services/defence/caf/military-identity-system/rank-appointment-insignia.html.)

Becoming and remaining culturally savvy with respect to our Veteran clientele means that we stay committed to ongoing learning about programs and services, methods and practices, research, and information available. It means that we:

- Help our clients create a new/different sense of purpose as they transition to civilian life. What are the values they want to hold on to or prioritize at this life juncture? This will help them set a firm foundation on which to build their career and employment goals.

- Connect them with supportive networks. Veterans who have already transitioned or those still seeking employment can offer a safe space for sharing and mentorship.

- Offer virtual counselling or flexible hours. Whether stationed in Canada or overseas, being able to access our services virtually or during off-hours shows our Veteran clients that we are committed to accommodating them. And for those who consider asking for help a sign of weakness, being able to access user-friendly resources online can help them feel more confident.

Elaine Piper (a now-retired career development consultant introduced back in Chapter 3) offers some practical suggestions that, if implemented, can help the Veteran ease potential transition woes.

- By increasing their knowledge of and proficiency at using social media and creating a well-thought-out LinkedIn profile, transitioning members can start networking and making connections long before they leave service. That will enable them to "hit the ground running" once they transition. This is particularly true for those posted overseas and looking to relocate.

- They should get comfortable with video meetings/virtual platforms like Microsoft Teams or Zoom as these may be used for online interviews and/or consultations.

- Know their skills and what they have to offer. Keep track of their accomplishments.

- Drafting a resumé or crafting interview responses using artificial intelligence (AI) can help you get started but use it wisely. AI only knows what you tell it. Understand that once you share information on a free platform it's out there, so don't share personal information.

- Create a new purpose. What is going to make you happy?

Piper recommends the following resources:

- **MNET** (https://caface-rfacace.forces.gc.ca/mnet-oesc/en/) is a military-to-civilian job translator tied to the National Occupational

Classification (NOC) that allows military members to enter their Military Occupational Structure Identification Code (MOSID) and generate a civilian equivalent. The site also includes a list of resources relevant to civilian employment and employers including resumé-building tools.

- **My Skills and Education Translator (MySET)** (https://caface-rfacace. forces.gc.ca/en/index) provides a list of institutions will give credits for military training and experience.

- **The Conference Board of Canada's Employability Skills** (https:// www.conferenceboard.ca/future-skills-centre/tools/finding-your-em- ployability-skills/) describe those skills needed to succeed in the work world and are inclusive of social, emotional, self-management, and teamwork skills. Piper suggests having Veteran clients think about in which of these skills they are strongest.

- **The Government of Canada Job Bank** has a section for Veterans (https://www.jobbank.gc.ca/Veterans). Use this to learn about civilian equivalents, job search tools, and relevant resources.

One of the areas that bears remembering as we help clients clarify career goals or find work is that transitioning is a process and may include all the elements of the Job Loss Emotional Cycle.[53] It is important that we help Veterans understand that finding work will at times be frustrating, so they should prepare for the road ahead to have bad and good days, progress, and stagnant phases, before reaching the desired end goal.

Piper finds, from her experience working with Veterans, that reflection, for those wishing to engage, can be a powerful tool in the transition journey. Examining one's thoughts and feelings enables assessment of where we are coming from, what we've learned, and what to incorporate from that into future goals. Because purpose is and has been a huge component of the service member's ethos, any tool that will help them create a new sense of purpose will likely be meaningful. Use of journaling, recordings, dream boards, transition theories, collages or such is recommended. (See Appendix 1 for Piper's Reflection Exercise.)

Robert Miles offers a few complementary suggestions we can use in our work with transitioning military clients or Veterans:[54]

- **Assess career decision-making readiness**: Next to finding employment, the other pressing need of the Veteran is overcoming barriers. Some of these barriers are personal—a result of mental health or physical injuries. Some are systemic or societal. Is the client ready to proceed with career decision-making?

- **Assess interests and options**: What are the motivators for this client? Through interest inventories, storytelling, or other tools, the client can evaluate activities in their military occupations or leisure pursuits that they enjoyed and begin to see energizing possibilities.

- **Assess skills**: Helping Veteran clients determine the importance of their motivated skills (high interest + high proficiency) as opposed to their unmotivated skills (low interest + high proficiency) will help them design effective resumés and prepare for job interviews.

- **Assess changes in values**: Sometimes military service can have a drastic impact on the Veteran's values. Sorting easy-to-manipulate Values Cards can allow Veterans to compare how and what values have shifted, from then to now. Sometimes the shift means a change in their worldview. For example, "recognition" or "status" used to mean a lot. Now the focus might be on "security" or "stability." This provides an opportunity for the Veteran to vocalize feelings or thoughts and provides us with useful information on their core priorities.

- **Assist in decision-making**. Career practitioners can help clients separate short-term from long-term goals. What are factors for immediate consideration? Family issues, financial challenges, education? Helping clients sift through and determine their most pressing priorities at this stage is so very important.

- **Assist in implementation**. Often, this is where we lose our clients and where they need the most support. During the assessment phase of career counselling, clients are, for the most part, recipients of information. We provide them with results from whatever battery of inventories we have asked them to complete and help them see patterns and possibilities. At this implementation juncture, however, the client must take action. The proverbial ball is back in their court. (That's why determining readiness is such a critical step.)

For the client whose immediate priority is to find employment, the next step is active job searching. That means lots of networking, securing informational interviews, attending job fairs, facing possible rejection and employer biases, and keeping one's spirits up. Similarly, those who have opted for further education or training can benefit from our expertise in helping them navigate the landscape of civilian education—applications, credit transfers, accommodation (if needed), course selection, financial aid, and so on.

With that being said, let's move on to Part II, on employment and employability.

YVONNE'S FAVOURITES

◎ **Supporting Military Members in Career Transition** (https://registeratcontinuingeducation.dal.ca/search/publicCourseSearchDetails.do?method=load&courseId=77245). This certificate for career practitioners covers the following topics: Military Careers and Culture; Transition to Civilian Life and Work; Transferrable Skills; Job Search and Tools; Special Considerations. Note: The program is currently being redesigned by the Nova Scotia Career Development Association (https://www.nscda.ca) and will be offered as a fully self-directed eLearning component on their member training portal.

PART II

Employment and Employability

"A Network of Support"

If Kevin wrote a manifesto, it would be edgy and a bit dark, but the story would embody discipline, integrity, and excellence. After hitting rock bottom, so to speak, these are the values that now undergird his life as an entrepreneur, a husband, a dad, and a citizen. And also support. Kevin is convinced that the tapestry of his life would be so very different if not for the support of his wife and folks with whom he can be totally honest.

Kevin's decision to join the CAF was practical: He did not graduate high school and his stepdad, who had spent five years in the military, recommended it. On investigation he found that as a combat engineer he had the choice of many options in the military trades. So at 18 years old, he joined up. By the time he was 19, he was deployed to Afghanistan, where he learned to have fun while walking 15 kilometres per day alongside fear. He next did a tour in Ukraine, but after eight years of being hypervigilant every day, he was diagnosed with PTSD. At that time, his partner advised him to seek help, but like a true soldier, he soldiered on, intent on pushing through.

In 2018 Kevin was medically released due to escalating anger management issues. Because he had not finished high school, he did not know what to do, and the nature of the work he had done while in service had made him so hypervigilant he became extremely depressed and suicidal, neglecting his health and appearance. Afraid to even go outside, he felt trapped. So just to change things up, Kevin decided to grow a beard. That did not go well. The beard made his skin itchy, dry, and flaky. Unable to find products on the market to address this problem, he and his wife ended up starting their own business making skin-friendly products.

"Taking care of my appearance had a massive impact on my mental health," Kevin says. Developing products that would help others and having for himself a new "bearded" persona gave him a purpose. His company became one of the first Veteran-owned companies to sell products to the CAF and they managed that within six months of operation. But that's not all. Kevin formed a new community with fellow Veterans and other ex-servicemen that gave him a new mission and team. Uniforms, analytical skills, discipline—all elements learned in the military, he has been able to integrate into the business. "We push ourselves to be better in our jobs."

Kevin's business created its own ambassador program, a team built along the lines of military structure but with a difference. "We are all vulnerable. My role is giving them permission that it's okay to be vulnerable."

Kevin's biggest military-to-civilian-transition challenge was the not knowing. He did not know that the skills he had learned in the military were transferrable to becoming an entrepreneur. "Lots of Veterans don't know what they have," he states with regret. For him, being comfortable with the uncomfortable, remaining mission critical, being okay with stress, and believing that a way can always be found to overcome any obstacle and get the job done—all these are key to being a successful entrepreneur. These also are his best lessons learned since transition: "Be adaptable and persistent. There is a way around the problem. You just got to be creative."

Kevin would love to see more financial support for Veteran entrepreneurs. While there is funding for Veterans who want to go to school, he believes those like him who are not academically inclined have no access (via the military) to funds to help start a business.

His advice to those transitioning is as follows:

- ✓ Connect to a new network of support—a team that will energize and empower you.

- ✓ Be honest with people.

- ✓ Have people in your corner with whom you can have real talks and no judgement.

- ✓ Make sure you're not scared of asking for help. "I can't care more about you than you care about yourself."

"Lot of vets don't like "thanks for your service,'" Kevin notes in closing. "It is meant as a sign of respect but it makes them cringe. It was their job, so just be aware that they often don't know how to react to that."

And these words encapsulate the sentiment of his heart: "If I had been on my own, without the support, I would not be where I am."

CHAPTER 6

Finding Employment – The Challenges

CHAPTER CONTENTS

- ❧ What Veterans have to offer
- ❧ Where Veterans may struggle

Veterans Have Much to Offer, But...

Much has been documented, especially for employer audiences, to highlight the qualities and skills former soldiers, sailors, airmen, and airwomen bring to the workplace. Employers are seeking candidates who, in addition to having job-specific skills, are adaptable, flexible, self-motivated, dependable, reliable, committed, professional, mission-focused, and enthusiastic. Those who have been trained in military service possess these qualities and more:

- **Loyalty, dedication, and a sense of duty**: will stick with the task, no matter the hardship, until the mission is accomplished.

- **Teamwork/co-operation**: know how to work together for a common goal and trust each other to do what will ensure the success of the mission.

- **Leadership**: have been instructed in methods of managing, training, evaluating, and developing staff; know how to have people follow them because they believe in them.

- **Problem solving**: have been trained to find the optimal solution to a problem and are prepared to discard a planned course of action as the situation changes, all while working under pressure and in circumstances where the stakes are extremely high.

- **Discipline**: have been trained to keep body and mind—everything from one's kit to personal grooming and mental and physical fitness—in top shape. Failure to do so might result in loss of the right to wear the uniform.

- **Knowledge of people**: know how to train, manage, command, and gain respect.

- **Goal orientation/Mission focus**: have been taught that the need of the mission overrides the need of the self.

- **Responsibility**: are responsible for the lives of others, expensive equipment, or financial allocations.

- **Knowledge**: know how to operate communication systems and complex machinery, comply with safety standards, and pay attention to the smallest detail.

Given these more-than-stellar characteristics and skills, why then do many experience difficulties finding and adjusting to civilian employment?

Lack of Knowledge about Civilian Work Culture and Language

Imagine what it might be like for someone who for the past 10 or 15 years has lived in a completely different culture. In a very real sense, this is what it is like for service personnel who are transitioning to civilian careers. They experience culture shock. As noted before, a military member's priority is first the mission, then the team, and finally the self. In civilian work culture, this is reversed. The civilian job seeker must point out to the prospective employer how he himself can help the organization achieve its mission or how she herself will add value to the organization. This requires a completely opposite mindset.

Those of us who advise clients on the logistics of navigating the civilian job market know that it can be challenging even for the savvy job seeker. That's why we offer individualized coaching, counselling, or workshops to help clients learn the "tricks of the trade" and the language of the employer. We stress the importance of goal clarification and self-promotion, prepare our clients for behavioural and situational interview questions, and strongly advise them to do their market research.

Why? Because it is necessary for success!

Our Veteran client is moving from a predominantly hierarchical, conformist environment with clearly defined roles and career progression to one that rewards self-promotion and self-reliance. Therefore, she must take time to understand the differences in the new versus the former work culture and the requirements needed to succeed here.

Lucy, one of the Veterans profiled in this guide, had to adjust to matching her clothes. It's a simple thing, but when you've worn a uniform for most of your career, matching clothes can be a challenge. Alberto had to get used to the slower pace of work, and Marcel had to adjust to losing a piece of his identity that was tied to being "that military guy." No wonder they all advise early planning, even when they themselves did not do it. A soldier would never go into a mission without doing the necessary reconnaissance, or "recce." The same is true when entering or re-entering the civilian workplace—especially after a long absence.

Not only is there a difference in work cultures, but there can also be a language barrier. Military speech can be hard to understand for those not used to it. Moreover, acronyms and initialisms abound in military language. If you notice your client using a lot of military acronyms, explain that most of the civilian working world will not understand them and don't shy away from asking your client to provide translation using simple, non-military words. This might initially prove difficult for some but it is a necessary part of the transition.

It's our job to help our clients readjust their thinking so they can confidently describe, in language that's clear, how the culture and experiences of the military equipped them to be solid contributors to any organization.

Difficulty Articulating and Translating Skills

The how-to of translating military skills into civilian nomenclature and using this information to build stronger, more competitive resumés and cover letters is another area where career practitioners can assist military members and Veterans. Start by asking simple questions:

- What skills did you use in your military job?

- If you were training your replacement, what would you want them to know and be able to do?

- What did you need to do to complete a successful mission?

Sometimes clients have difficulty stepping back from what they've done for years to see and describe it objectively. When this happens, we could have them walk us through a typical day on the job, asking for details as they do so. (Note that, given its nature, some work done by our clients they are not at liberty to discuss.)

Clients whose postings included a number of different roles and tasks—where they had to learn an entirely new job, master it, and evolve it before moving on—have an important competence we could help them leverage.

A Veteran who, for example, was an Infantry Officer for 25 years, may have held jobs akin to that of a Senior Manager, HR Manager, Supply Manager, or Financial Manager over the course of those 25 years. One approach might be to ask the Veteran: "When you think about your military career, what posting(s) are you most proud of?" As we listen, we take notes, documenting the skills we see at work. In working with former members of the military, especially those who worked in roles very different from any civilian equivalent, this "drawing out" process is critical.

So pull out those career card decks. Card-playing works especially well with clients who are more comfortable doing than speaking. Sorting Skills Cards can help clients see what they have done, what they want to continue doing, and/or in which areas they want to develop.

If, however, your client is coming from a difficult job experience, he may be feeling shaky about his skills. Maybe he was terminated or has been job searching for a while with little success. By now, self-doubt has crept in. Alternatively, if a client has been in combat, there is a high probability that her values might have shifted.[55] In these situations, instead of starting with a skills-identification exercise, using Values Cards can be more effective.

Values can be compared to the foundation of a house. They tell us about the things that anchor the client. If you are meeting with the client in person, carefully observe how they play the cards. Do they make quick decisions, hesitate a lot, converse with themselves as they go through the exercise, or employ other behaviours? That's the first step. Next, ask them to group their "Strongly valued" cards by theme. Based on your sense of the client, you can challenge some of their card placements, but mostly you want to see how their mind works. Finally, have them select 10 to 12 values that they want the next segment of their lives to embody. It is amazing how telling this process can be—to them and to us.

If you are meeting with the client virtually, you can sort the cards on their behalf. You can be their hands and they the brains. Then send them photographs of the cards at each segment of the exercise until you get to the end. Some clients find it challenging to download and re-orient the photos as sent, but see this as a training opportunity in getting them comfortable with virtual competencies.

Whether you start with Skills or with Values, these simple exercises (or any other self-assessment exercise you know and love) should help the ex–military member get at what they have to offer and the guiding principles that undergird their choices. (Note: Career practitioner Dwayne Cormier has worked extensively with military members and has found that the COPSystem is typically the most well-received assessment by his clients. See link reference later in this chapter.)

Civilian Myths and Misperceptions

Opinions about war and warfare abound. The life of a soldier—the work, training, military experiences, and history—makes some people nervous. News items dwelling on the negative aspects of military culture shape our perspectives, even as career practitioners. And without knowing it, we internalize a belief.

An employer who sees on a resumé that an applicant has served a tour of duty in Ukraine, Syria, or wherever and begins to wonder if there is cause for alarm could be reacting out of an internalized belief that may or may not be true. Does this applicant have a post-traumatic stress disorder? Will he require all kinds of accommodation on the job? Will she be a drain on resources? Will he (if a Reservist) be called up again? Already the candidate is being judged as a potential liability.

One Veteran I spoke with said that he and his peers often elect not to talk about their military careers except to those who've been through it.

How then do our clients tap into their vast military experience without making people nervous?

Of course, employers have an obligation to hire the best candidates to meet the workforce needs of their organizations. But… is this employer acting from a place of conscious or subconscious bias? If yes, she may be turning away a potentially stellar employee, sight unseen.

Challenge Factory explored the topic of employer bias in a study done in 2018.[56] They posed the following three questions to a group of employers:

1. Are Veterans different than the typical civilian employees?

2. Are Veterans different from what employers believe about them?

3. If yes to the above, how are they different?

An interesting component of the study was the use of personas. Employer participants were asked to answer a set of questions, not as themselves, but from a self-constructed persona perspective. This allowed the employer to enter into the experience of job-seeking Veterans and resulted in increased empathy and understanding.

We need more of these kinds of challenges! By treating each Veteran as an individual, persisting in raising awareness and advocating on their behalf, much can be done to minimize the misperceptions that negatively impact hiring practices.

Lack of Awareness

Every year, on the first Sunday in June, Canada celebrates Canadian Armed Forces Day. In areas where there is a strong CAF presence, one typically finds more community partnerships and support. In large, urban settings the CAF presence is more diffuse. Remembrance Day events and activities continue to be meaningful in raising civilian awareness about the sacrifices of CAF members and Veterans. In addition, Veterans Affairs Canada, the CAF, and other organizations are committed to educating employers about the benefits of hiring former military members.

Not Knowing Civilian Job Equivalents

Let's say you are working with someone who served as an Infantry Soldier in the CAF. As a member of a focused and disciplined team, these soldiers are responsible for combat duties. They must be able to endure all extremes of climate and weather conditions, deal with stress and deprivation, understand and execute orders, and live in close, cramped quarters. They must also be able to carry their Field and Fighting Order kits weighing between 35 and 44 kg.

How would you help this client find work? What civilian jobs do you think this person could do?

Become familiar with MNET, a military-to-civilian job translation tool (https://caface-rfacace.forces.gc.ca/mnet-oesc/en/). On the MNET site, your client can enter her Military Occupational Structure Identification Code (MOSID) to generate a list of civilian job equivalents.

In our example, the search for "Infantryman" on MNET generated a number of possibilities ranging from human resources to logistics, cleaning, and construction, to name a few. As with the advanced search parameters of the National Occupational Classification (NOC) or other inventories, not all of the titles generated may align with careers of interest for your client. We can now ask our client to tell us, in greater detail (if she is comfortable) what her military job entailed. From the Infantryman job description, teamwork, mission focus, mental fortitude, and grit are obvious. Once we hear from the client which components of that work she enjoyed and thrived in, we can use our expertise to help her hone in on potential civilian career pathways—security, cybersecurity (if she is technically adept), team leadership, law enforcement, correctional officer, trainer, etc.

But what if our former Infantry Soldier is not interested in any of the generated options or has no clue what she wants to do now?

This is when a more comprehensive assessment tool can be of benefit. You have your favourites that are tried and true. Use those. Here are a couple others worth looking into in case you are not familiar with them:

- **COPSystem** (https://www.edits.net/via) incorporates interests, abilities, and work values in generating occupations. Though linked to the American Occupational Information Network (O*NET), the COPSystem site does provide a National Occupational Classification (NOC) document where one can see Canadian career equivalents (https://copsystem.edits.net/public/ccg-c-wbb.pdf).

- The **Self-Directed Search® (SDS)** assessment report (https://self-directed-search.com/Veterans) provides interest results related to the Holland Codes. (Research has shown a predominance of Realistic, Investigative, Enterprising, and Social types in military occupations and personalities.) The report also shows civilian roles related to military skill sets, programs of study related to Holland Codes, salary information, a transition planning checklist, and more.

Note: COPSystem and SDS are both US tools but can be useful as alternatives in generating civilian occupations. At the time of this writing, a digital COPSystem report costs US$12.00 and a customized SDS costs US$18.95.

Another useful resource is the Government of Canada Job Bank for Veterans (https://www.jobbank.gc.ca/Veterans). Veterans can learn about civilian job equivalents, complete a skills and knowledge checklist, and view job search tools and other relevant resources.

Lack of Knowledge about Services Available

There is a wealth of services available to help CAF Veterans. As stated earlier, the CAF is moving toward a culture of change where transition planning begins on Day 1 in uniform. Transition will happen to 100% of serving personnel in one form or another during their time in service. The fact that transitioning Veterans now have between 6 months and 30 days to dedicate to transition planning is great. However, when there is a lot of work to get done prior to leaving, the military mindset of duty before self can kick in, so the member is not able to take the time needed to do the necessary transition planning work. We can help them learn about and navigate these services as we become familiar with them ourselves. Encourage transitioning members to avail themselves of the Career Transition Services (https://www.veterans. gc.ca/en/education-and-jobs/find-new-job/career-transition-services) and their Transition Advisors. Serving members as well as Veterans can also avail themselves of the VAC Transition Services (see https://www.veterans.gc.ca/ for a comprehensive list of services).

In CERIC's 2021 Career Development in the Canadian Workplace: National Business Survey, 75% of employers surveyed identified "a shortage of skilled workers" to be significantly or somewhat challenging for their organizations.[57] Tapping into the stellar skill set of transitioned or transitioning CAF members would be awesome, wouldn't it? But alas, there is no active process in place or military job developer resource to address this need. (Maybe someone reading this guide right now might want to tackle that next?)

In the interim, we can advocate amongst our employer colleagues about the excellent attributes and competencies CAF Veterans are able to bring to the civilian job market.

* * *

This completes the big-picture overview of finding civilian work. Now let's get down to the nitty-gritty of what can be done to help our clients address their employment needs.

★ The CAF instills in members many skills that civilian employers need.

★ Misperceptions about the military affect civilian attitudes, beliefs, and even hiring practices.

★ Resources are available to identify civilian equivalents to military jobs.

★ CAF members do not always know about the services available to help them in the transition to civilian life.

YVONNE'S FAVOURITES

◎ The **Government of Canada Job Bank** includes a skills and knowledge checklist (https://www.jobbank.gc.ca/career-planning/skills-knowledge) whereby job seekers can identify their skills from 10 categories and their knowledge from nine areas. Results yield a Skills and Knowledge Profile showing related occupations, skills matches, and knowledge needed. By clicking on the occupations, one can view all the current jobs available by region.

◎ **Digital Transition Center** (https://www.canada.ca/en/department-national-defence/services/benefits-military/transition.html). This resource includes virtual access to transition counselling, transition training, and education initiatives. Within the DTC, there is also My Skills and Education Translator (My SET) and MNET, which help in determining civilian equivalents to military occupations.

◎ **Military Transition Engagement and Partnerships (MTEP)** (https://www.canada.ca/en/department-national-defence/services/benefits-military/transition/mtep.html), a digital national network for organizations, businesses, and programs that support transitioning military/Veterans and their families.

"The opportunity I had to serve our great country was a great thing… so rewarding, and I'm so proud of our career."

—Chief Warrant Officer (Retired)

"Family Anchors"

At the ripe old age of 19, Charles joined the CAF Reserves. But it was not enough to be on the ground. His deep, deep passion was to be up in the air. As far back as he can recall, anything to do with aviation fascinated him. And so it was not surprising that when he discovered early in his university years that he did not need a degree to be a member of the Air Force, he quit the Reserves and university and enlisted in the Air Force through their Officer Candidate Program. He was on his way to the skies!

Of course it helped that the same year he joined, the movie *Top Gun* came out. How cool was that!

For Charles, to get to do what you love (flying) where the organization also looks after you, pays for your training, and allows you to gain experience and adventure was a dream come true. He would often come home and say to his wife, "I cannot believe they pay me to do what I'm doing." She, mired in holding down the fort at home, was not impressed.

It took almost 34 years before Charles made the decision to leave, retiring as a full-fledged Deputy Commander of the Air Force. With the exception of a few frustrating roles, the work for the most part was challenging and rewarding. "In hindsight," he says, "I can't think of a job that I did not enjoy." But at age 55, he felt it was time. He'd worked hard, made a difference, contributed, and "finished with the same spouse I started out with."

As he reflects on his life in the Air Force, Charles says he misses the people. "You grow attached to being around people who are like-minded and focused on the same things. You're part of a professional culture that kind of defines who you are." What he does not miss is the sometimes brutal pace of the work that went with it, especially toward the end of his tenure. Retirement allowed him to trade that sense of belonging and institutional attachment for the latitude of doing more of the things he wants to do, not has to do.

On his road to transitioning out, Charles recalls someone telling him that it was now time to become a human "being" and not just a human "doing." "I do not consider myself busy now. I am occupied with the things I want to do. And now we (the family) get to do many of the things we want to do."

The decision to leave was deliberate. "I provided nine months' notice. Most people don't do that." He remembers well how hard it was to make formal his intentions to retire. "But each subsequent day became easier and easier. I had no choice now. I had told them. Now I had to figure it out."

The other thing that helped the transition was that he and his family made a conscious decision about what they were going to do immediately following his retirement (travel). "It gave me something to look forward to and being away for that extended period of time (one month) really created a break."

For Charles, the biggest adjustment post-service was his schedule, or lack thereof. "I am incapable of managing a schedule. I was so busy before I retired, hyperfocused on schedule—had two staff who managed my largely set schedule for each day. I just moved from one thing to the next. Now I have to find something to do in the 50–55 hours per week."

Just over one year out, Charles considers his life to be much more balanced now. His current job as a consultant allows him to maintain some connection with the CAF but on his terms.

What advice would he give to someone leaving? "You have to make a decision based on your terms. Do it because it is something you want. If you leave anything in life bitter, that's where the difficulty really comes in. You've got to make a conscious decision that this is that right thing to do for you and you are doing it for you, not because you feel mistreated or based on something the organization has said and done. If you can rationalize and come to that point, it will make the transition easier."

Charles offers this advice based on his observations of people who have left. Those who felt forced out or felt cheated by the system, so to speak, carried with them a sense of bitterness. He believes that whatever the circumstances of the departure, one has get to a place that allows them to make peace with what they have done. Taking the long view, with a good attitude and a positive outlook, is key to surviving life without bitterness.

Additional advice, insights, observations from Charles:

✓ Spouses that succeed at military life are the ones who figure out just how to get on with it regardless of what is happening. Mindset and attitude are really important.

✓ We always took the attitude with our children that there is a big difference between a house and a home. House is a physical structure; home is what we do with the physical structure—what we do in it, how we come together, how we enjoy each other's company. It didn't matter where we lived. It's what we do in it that matters.

✓ The transition experience is highly personal and very individual. The people who are successful at it are probably the majority of those who leave voluntarily and are ready to do something else. The ones that really struggle are those who are leaving because they have to, don't want to, or don't know what they are going to do on the other side.

✓ The transition experience is very process-driven. Right now, it's a one-size-fits-all system, and there needs to be a trained advisor at the outset who can identify which transitioning members are in trouble and will need more help during the process of getting to the point of readiness and peace with the decision.

✓ There's a very different culture between the military and most of the private sector. For most in the private sector, it is a job, but the military is much more a way of life that transcends the Monday-to-Friday aspect. I don't think many people understand that. In the military, you got to be part of something bigger. Transitioning members are looking for that same kind of attachment/bigger purpose.

✓ Do not take the first job thrown at you. Make sure that it is what you want.

"As I look back on my 34 years, one of the defining highlights of my career is the fact that I retired with the same wife I started with. I tell everyone that my definition of success in a career is twofold: (1) that you felt you had contributed and made a difference to the institution you were working in, and (2) equally as important, you had done it in a way that allowed you to have a family and relationships outside of that institution. The family has been an incredible frame against which I've been able to do the things that I have."

CHAPTER 7

Finding Employment – Tools and Resources

The dominant need of transitioning members is to define a new identity and sense of purpose in the civilian world. For some, this means finding meaningful work. The Veteran whose mindset cannot conceive of sitting around and doing nothing might be tempted to jump on the first job that sounds good only to find out a few months in that it is not really for them. Taking time to get a clear picture of the kind of work that will satisfy is so very necessary. It can be likened to creating an objective, planning a mission, or shooting a target. Success is meeting the objective, completing the mission, or securing the target.

Let's consider the former Infantry Soldier we met in Chapter 6. In order to secure a job, she will need to identify the things needed in a career to make it meaningful, have a fairly clear job goal, know the skills she has to offer, have an effective resumé, collect job leads/connections, prepare for interviews, etc. This is her new mission.

Core Values and Attributes

For the Veteran client looking to create a work life outside the CAF, something that will give them a new sense of identity and purpose, it is critical in my opinion to spend some time working on values. Values assessment allows them to take stock and to focus on the core things needed to make this chapter of their life meaningful.

What lies at the heart of what they want to focus on now?

After years working as a career practitioner, I am still amazed at how telling a values assessment can be for clients. So... pull out your values card sorts or any other kind of work/life values inventory and gently guide the client to identify the ones they want the work they do post-military to embody. This will definitely help them to know what to look for in a job or company and what to ask for during the interview.

And while we are on the subject of values, let's remember to incorporate relevant attributes into the value-add our clients bring to the job. A person who is analytical, detail-oriented, visionary, co-operative, methodical, or whatever the attribute will be much happier in a job that utilizes their personality attributes and aligns with their core values. As Blake, one of our profilees, said, "When looking for civilian employment, pay attention to the values of the company you want to work with."

Clarity

It happens all the time. The client schedules an appointment to have you help her find a job. You ask the question—what kind of job are you looking for? And sometimes you get an answer like this, "Anything, just a job."

Really now!

On days when I'm feeling particularly mischievous or cranky, I randomly pick a job for them to do. Suddenly they start providing criteria—"I don't like that," "I can't do that," or "I wish!" From their responses to the randomly assigned job, we can teach them why "any job" will obviously not do.

We cannot effectively help clients who have no clear idea of what they want to do. Without a clear job goal, one is really flying blind, hoping to land safely. It can be done, but the stress is acute. There is not enough time in the world for clients to try out all the career possibilities available, so our job is to help them clarify what kind of work they are looking for. Do they want to do work similar to what they did in the CAF or do they want to make a complete career change?

If the client wishes to do work similar or compatible to that done while in service, the MNET tool is a great place to start as is the CAF recruiting website (https://www.forces.ca/). Using these, they can generate a list of career possibilities and, from that list, identify the ones that are most compatible with their skills and aptitudes.

If, on the other hand, the client wishes to make a complete career change and does not know what he wants, those of us who are skilled career counsellors may be better equipped to help here. This is where we guide the client through a career self-assessment process—identifying skills (have or want to learn), values, attributes, ideal work environment, and interests, using standardized assessment inventories, to create a career profile. The client can then use the information learned as a rubric to determine alignment with different career options.

In situations where the client cannot come up with a clear goal, brainstorming can also be useful. We can ask them to describe an activity they enjoy or to tell us about the kinds of tasks they are good at. Other questions include: What do people ask for your help with? What are you doing when you feel the most energized and authentic? What aspects of your former job did you love/hate? Any of these can provide clues we can use to guide the client into a new role direction.

But be prepared: Even when you do all the above, some clients just cannot seem to muster up any enthusiasm for anything. That's when you know that other factors are at work. Depression, anxiety, "stuckness," trauma, and fear can all contribute to this inability to see oneself in a new role. We can gently probe to find out what may be contributing to this and direct the client to seek professional assistance before moving forward. This is where the National Resource Directory (https://military-transition.canada.ca/en/national-resource-directory) can be useful for connecting them with trusted health care providers.

Veteran Affairs Canada also has several Benefits and Services https://www.veterans.gc.ca/en/news-and-media/infographics/our-benefits-and-services that may be available to qualifying Veterans. Veterans in need of services or assistance can contact Veterans Affairs Canada at **1-866-522-2122 (English)** or **1-866-522-2022 (French)**.

Skills

Skills assessment is an important step—a necessary component of the "tooling" process. For the fictitious Infantry Soldier we have been discussing, the challenge might be in identifying which of her skills are relevant to the type of civilian work she wants to do. By having the client perform a transferability skills checklist, or by using your favourite skills-assessment exercise, you will ensure she not only knows what she has to offer, but can also clearly articulate and illustrate her skills during a job interview (more on that to come).

Remember, the CAF provides excellent training in skills that are transferable to the civilian workplace in three areas: (1) **interpersonal** – working as part of a team; (2) **leadership** – how to command, lead, guide, and mentor; and (3) **technical** – skills learned in one's trade or profession. Many CAF members are also trained at the same recognized civilian institutions as their counterparts without military service. Veterans also demonstrate valued qualities like responsibility, reliability, and a "get it done" attitude. Therefore, the more we can get our clients to tap into these areas of strength, the more we are speaking their language.

Personally, I have found that grouping skills into categories helps the client see patterns or themes to what they have done. These themes can help them hone in on areas of motivation, which can in turn provide good fodder for resumé-building. For example, let's say that the client has identified a list of 15 skills that he's good at and enjoys using, and the list looks like this:

- Teamwork
- Helping others
- Teaching/training/instructing
- Organization
- Planning
- Coordinating
- Problem solving
- Evaluating (quantitative and qualitative)
- Research
- Supervision
- Leadership

- Crisis management

- Motivating

- Communication

You will notice that three main categories can be derived from this list: **relational skills** (teamwork, helping, teaching/training, motivating, leadership, supervising, communication); **organizational skills** (organizing, planning, coordinating, supervising); and **analytical skills** (problem solving, research, evaluating, crisis management). Our client can then ensure that these categories are highlighted on his resumé and can, in advance, think through examples of where he has used these skills in the past and how they helped to accomplish the mission, add value, reduce costs/waste, increase efficiencies, etc.

This exercise can further help the client identify jobs that require the skill sets that he wants to use in work.

The Resumé

Chronological, functional (skill based), or a combination—the resumé is still the tool of choice to communicate one's qualifications for a job. From a military culture perspective, it is important to understand that military personnel are used to "wearing" a huge part of their resumé. Everything on the uniform signifies a substantial amount of information about a military career. For example, the cap badge tells the occupation; the rank, the level of responsibility; the medals, the specific types of experiences and time in uniform; various commendation pins and other accoutrements separate high performers from others; etc.

While not every aspect of a military person's resumé is on the uniform, a lot of it is. This is one of the reasons military personnel are not well versed in translating military experiences into words on a resumé: they are used to it being seen and understood, without having to be explained.

The newly minted Veteran coming to us for help in finding civilian employment likely will know that she needs a written resumé. Our job, after getting to know her and her employment and educational history, is to help her build the strongest possible case for herself about what she can contribute to an organization and teach her how to document this on paper and articulate it in an interview. There is no uniform to "read," and even if there were, not many civilian employers would know how.

For the Veteran client, we want to ensure that the resumé is not riddled with military jargon and that her experience and skills are clearly articulated. AI technology can help with format, layout, templates, and wording, but an astute career practitioner can help hone in on what is critical to communicate about herself in language that the target audience can understand.

The sample military resumé in Appendix 3 illustrates how military experience can be communicated to a civilian employer for the fictional Mason Cummings, an IT professional. By including areas of expertise right up front, he communicates his competencies in language relevant to the industry he's targeting. Of course, it would be advisable that Mason spell out the acronyms used beside his name to ensure the qualifications he wants highlighted are clearly understood. Another thing to fix would be consistency in language and formatting—for example, in all areas of his work and education he specifies the duration of time, but did not do so for his bachelor's degree. There he listed what may be the year of graduation but which could also imply that he finished the bachelor's degree in one year. In one employment entry, he uses the terms "Commanding Officer" and "Officer Commanding," and it is not clear if these mean the same thing. There are a few other minor inconsistencies or editorial details that can be improved, but I will leave those for you to discover. Overall though, the resumé nicely documents his military experience and its relevance to his current employment pursuit.

When we advise our clients on resume building, we also want to remind them why flagging areas of expertise is useful for cases where AI or Application Tracking Systems are employed to select candidates meeting job requirements. Targeting the language of the resumé to exactly reflect the skills, experiences, education, or certifications the employer is looking for is also good practice.

Case in point: I once had a staff member give notice to leave her job during an especially busy time for my department. I needed to post and fill the job ASAP. The day following the application deadline, when I went to check the applicant pool, I discovered over 400+ resumés for the one position. No one, myself included, wants to go through such a daunting list, plus I definitely did not have the time. So what I did was use a series of filters to flag only the resumés that met all of the job requirements.

Finally, applicants should demonstrate that they are connected and current with social media.

These are examples of small but important tips career practitioners can offer to help transitioning military members ensure their resumés are civilian-workplace ready.

Jobs Leads/Connections

With the prevalence of job boards it is easy for our clients to post their resumés online and feel that they are "actively" looking for work. Most realize quite quickly that the return on investment is slim. Connections and networks are a critical component of job-finding. But where can our transitioning members establish connections when they have not been in the civilian world for a while or spent all their working life in the CAF?

Almost all of the men and women profiled in this guide recommend connecting with those who have already transitioned. These connections speak the same language, understand the stresses of transition, and have words of wisdom to share. Our job is to encourage our clients in making these connections, if they have not already done so. Veteran Blake (profiled next), conducted over 30 informational interviews with people working in areas of interest. All the jobs he secured directly resulted from those connections.

We can tell our clients to start by creating a LinkedIn profile. They can also reach out to LinkedIn groups or other Veteran networks (see Chapter 3, Support Networks for At-risk Transitioning Members/Veterans, and Chapter 12, Employment).

Veterans want to help other Veterans. Let's encourage our clients to network and teach them how to do it well.

Selected Employment Resources

Job-training services, links to military-friendly employers, online networks, retraining subsidies, job listings, transition planning, resumé and job search help are available to transitioning members and Veterans. Some of these services can be accessed before one leaves the military so that adequate pre-planning can be done. Here are a few key services:

Digital Transition Centre

https://www.canada.ca/en/department-national-de-
fence/services/benefits-military/transition.html

This resource includes virtual access to transition counselling, transition training, and education initiatives. Within the DTC, there is also My Skills and Education Translator (My SET) and MNET, which can provide assistance in determining civilian equivalents for military occupations.

Military Transition Engagement & Partnerships (MTEP)

https://www.canada.ca/en/department-national-de-
fence/services/benefits-military/transition/mtep.html

A digital national network for organizations, businesses, and programs that support transitioning military/Veterans and their families. Organizations or service providers supportive of the military, Veteran, and family communities can join by going to the MTEP landing page and submitting a registration to join the National Resource Directory (NRD). Once in the NRD, organizations will also be able to share best practices with each other about how to support military members, Veterans, and their families.

Veterans Affairs Canada (CTS)

https://www.Veterans.gc.ca/en/education-and-jobs/
prepare-release/career-transition-services

Veterans Affairs Canada's Career Transition Services provide a comprehensive support system for qualifying Canadian Armed Forces members, Veterans, spouses/partners, and survivors inclusive of one-on-one career counselling, resume writing assistance, interview preparation, labour market information and analysis, and job search support. In addition, the Rehabilitation Services and Vocational Assistance Program (RSVP) offers a suite of medical, psycho-social, and vocational rehabilitation services to eligible Veterans.

Canadian Armed Forces Career Transition Centres

https://www.canada.ca/en/department-national-de-
fence/services/benefits-military/transition.html

Provides assistance with second careers, career transition workshops, a vocational program for serving members, referrals to sources of employment within the federal Public Service, toolkits, and more.

The Canadian Guide to Hiring Veterans

https://www.challengefactory.ca/VeteranHiringGuide

The Canadian Guide to Hiring Veterans is an easy-to-use publication that helps employers find, hire, and retain Veterans. Veterans can use the guide to identify organizations that are hiring.

Government of Canada Job Bank: For Veterans

https://www.jobbank.gc.ca/Veterans

This national database offers job listings, career exploration tools, and job market news to transition Veterans to meaningful careers. They have helped military members enter the post-military workforce for over 100 years.

How to Hire a Veteran

https://www.veterans.gc.ca/en/education-and-jobs/find-new-job/jobs-Veterans/employers-seeking-hire-Veterans

This VAC web page seeks to connect prospective employers and Veterans. It includes a registration form for employers and the link to create a company account with Employment and Social Development Canada's Job Bank.

True Patriot Love Veteran Hub

https://www.veteranhub.ca/

This hub is a one-stop shop where Veterans, military members, and their families can find volunteering opportunities, events, and services in their local community. It also has options for additional programs/events to be added to the hub, to keep the information as up-to-date as possible.

VAC Hire A Veteran LinkedIn Group

https://www.linkedin.com/groups/12536921/

This is a private LinkedIn group connecting transitioning military members and Veterans with employers that put an emphasis on hiring Veterans for skills they gained through military service.

The Interview

All career practitioners have within our toolkits tried and proven interview tips. In addition to the pre-interview basics—research the organization, determine values alignment, ensure the resumé is job-ready, line up references, choose appropriate attire—the novice Veteran job searcher will likely require more than one interview prep session.

Because they come from a work culture where performance and seniority form the basis for promotions, where promotions are likely initiated at the recommendation of one's commanding officer, and where self-promotion is not a core value, Veterans are understandably not used to, or even comfortable with, the idea of selling themselves.

Without trying to tell career professionals like you how to do your job, I present these questions for consideration:

- How will we prepare our clients to address employer skepticism about their ability (or willingness) to adapt to a civilian work culture?

- How will we teach our clients to speak knowledgeably about the added value they bring to an organization?

- What tips will we offer to help our clients describe how their military background has equipped them with skills that can meet an employer's needs? What would we do, for example, to encourage a Veteran client to describe the scope of his responsibility when at a young age he might have managed a number of people or a budget far exceeding that of a similar-aged civilian counterpart?

- How will we do these things with a client who has been steeped in a culture where the mission has priority over the self?

Suggestions for Practitioners

As you can see, there are many employment resources available to Veterans. Sometimes, however, in the course of our work with a particular client group, we discover a missing component or a gap. If that's the case, partner with an existing military-oriented service provider, where possible, to bring that added component to fruition instead of trying to create yet one more separate resource for Veterans to discover.

It is the welcoming approach, the understanding we demonstrate, the willingness to listen, the respect, and step-by-step guidance that are needed and treasured. With that in mind, permit me to offer a few more suggestions:

- Have your military clients register with the CAF and VAC Career Transition Services if they have not already done so. This group is 100% dedicated to helping with the transition to civilian life.

- Focus on helping your clients identify the skills, personal attributes, values, and experiences that will help them land a job.

- Offer virtual options for clients to connect with you.

- Provide customized and individualized career coaching/counselling tailored to meet the unique needs of your military client. Each is different.

- Get to know the resources that are available to assist with support, training, education, and employment.

- Learn which organizations are Veteran friendly.

- Get to know other career practitioners who can share information as well as best practices in working with transitioning military members.

- Participate in events or activities for transitioning military members to keep your knowledge up-to-date.

***

Now that we are more aware of the military-to-civilian-employment landscape, what we have not yet addressed—and need to, based on experience—is the reality that even though our clients may be anxious to find work, for some, the need for further education/training, mental challenges, or physical challenges stand between them and their desired goal. We also know we are not equipped to be all things to all people. That's why we keep as current as we can on programs, service providers, initiatives, tools, and strategies. Our knowledge is one of our best commodities.

So let's move to the next chapter. There we will explore things we can do to help clients overcome transitional barriers to employment.

KEY LEARNING

★ Transitioning military clients need help clarifying goals, identifying skills, writing resumés, preparing for interviews, and learning where to find work. And they need to be ready to make the change.

★ A number of career and employment programs and services are available to help transitioning Veterans look for and find work in different occupational areas.

★ Career practitioners should become familiar with what's out there and where possible, complement, not duplicate, already available resources.

Education and Training

"Approach each Veteran at face value. Not as a walking wounded. Level with them as humans. Not victims."

—That Military Guy

"Get Over Yourself"

Blake's military transition, since leaving in 2019, has been a long, exhausting, iterative, and educative process. His key learning in all the ups and downs was to let it go and to get over himself.

Blake joined the CAF when he was 19 as a private combat engineer in the Regular Forces. Hailing from a rural town in western Canada, the CAF seemed the only logical choice given his terrible grades and the fact that he'd begun getting into all kinds of trouble. His dad issued him an ultimatum. So he joined up, cognizant of the pros: job security, no stellar grades required, and the promise of a pension. He left in 2019, after serving close to 31 years, at the rank of Master Warrant Officer with the Special Forces.

The 31 years of service might have been fewer had the job he took after 10 years of service worked out. Too many moves, being away from family 200+ days a year, marital strain, three kids, a salary freeze, and the opportunity to make lots of money in the Alberta oil boom were contributing factors to his leaving. But within a week of starting the new job, the oil industry went bust and he was unemployed.

It took a year of doing odd jobs here and there before he was accepted back into service in 1999. Blake returned to the same job he had when he left but with a different unit and was medically released in 2019. He admits he would have stayed longer if not for his diagnosis of PTSD and post-concussive brain injury.

"There are three categories of releases," Blake says, "medical, retiring or when you've had enough. Each has different nuances and depends on which element you are retiring from—Army, Navy, Air Force or Special Forces."

Blake admits that he did not manage the transition well. At that time of his medical release, he felt unsupported, unconnected, and unaccountable. All he had to do was phone in once per week to the Transition Centre. "It was soul-sucking."

Remarried by this time, his wife "booted me in the ass." She reminded him that the Army owed him nothing and that he needed to get over himself and get on with life.

During that grey space of his transition, Blake got called back to Special Forces as an occupational stress injury coordinator. He was charged with interviewing colleagues about the barriers faced during transition and writing a report. That became part of his road to recovery. "It was good for me to do that. It was nice for me to come back before I left."

Since leaving, Blake has gotten certification in life coaching, attended four semesters of university studies, conducted multiple informational interviews, created a LinkedIn profile, and worked in many jobs those informational interviews connected him to—as an executive assistant, a health and safety trainer, and his current full-time role in security and construction deployment. It's a role that challenges him every day, pays well, and led him to the path of individuation. The key to securing employment was networking and connecting with other Veterans who had successfully transitioned.

Following his career as a non-commissioned officer (NCO), Blake spent time re-educating himself about himself and about the civilian job market. Although he had a substantial resumé with impressive experiences and accolades, he had few civilian qualifications. Blake quickly discovered that unless he found a workplace that had a person filtering resumés by reading them, he had little chance of being noticed with electronic job applications.

But the self-discovery process took even more time. "I never was my own person. I never knew who my personal self was. The era I grew up in the military, it was not easy to speak about your emotions. It took me a year to say out loud that I was angry. Because I was so immersed in my past life, letting it go took a while."

And that was the hardest part of his transition adjustment. "Individuation. Letting it go. Realizing that the military was not what I was. It was what I did."

Blake read a lot. Anything that could help him get over himself and come to terms with his new life, he devoured. (See below for his recommended books/resources.)

Blake's advice to transitioning members?

- ✓ Go get educated while you are in with something you can do after you get out.

- ✓ When looking for civilian employment, pay attention to the values of the company you want to work with.

- ✓ Network. Whether they are vets or just regular folk, you never know where these connections may lead.

- ✓ Let go of the military. "Once I let go and got over myself, it empowered me to take control of my transition and reintegration so I can shape my future with the values I brought from the military."

- ✓ Write your own Commander Intent. "Once you realize that you are writing your own commander intent [mission statement of the commander] for yourself now, that's a big deal."

- ✓ Allow yourself to grieve. "There's a grieving of loss—lost time, lost friends… allow yourself that time to grieve. That was a big deal to me—but very necessary."

Blake shares as his last words something his wife said that he had to humble himself to apply inwards, owning his mistakes, and reconciling with the past: "'Listening is fixing. It's my new lower back tattoo'—and his new mission statement.

Recommended books/resources

- *Beyond the Military: A Leader's Handbook for Warrior Reintegration* – Jason Roncoroni and Shauna Springer

- *Non-violent Communication* – Marshall B. Rosenberg

- *Codependent No More* – Melody Beattie

- *The Way of the Superior Man* – David Deida

- *Leaders Eat Last* – Simon Sinek

- *Start With Why* – Simon Sinek

- *Daring Greatly* – Brené Brown

- *I Don't Want to Talk about It* – Terrence Real

- Treble Victor – https://treblevictor.org (Members receive a Transition Assistance Aide document that is really useful.)

CHAPTER 8

Education and Training – Needs and Resources

Educating Employers

It was noted previously that employer myths and misconceptions about military service members can become a barrier to transition. Organizations like CAF TG and Veterans Affairs Canada are mandated to represent and advocate for the interest of Veterans in this arena. More to the point, the CAF encourages educational upgrading as part of professional development in one's military career.

In October 2023, the Standing Committee on Veterans Affairs released the National Strategy on Veteran Employment report, commissioned by Prime Minister Justin Trudeau. Recommendation 23 states, "That the Government of Canada, when developing its national strategy for Veterans' employment, encourage a dialogue between employers and Veterans in order to further mutual understanding and respect."[58]

The Veterans Employment Strategy, announced in June 2024, provides a "comprehensive roadmap to support Veteran employment by leveraging their unique qualifications… and we are committed to ensuring every Veteran has the opportunity to find meaningful employment."[59] This includes building relationships with both public- and private-sector employers to raise awareness of the competencies Veterans bring to the workplace. It should be noted as well that, according to 2021 Census data, almost 33% of Veterans are in that core working-age group of 25–54—primed to make an impact on the Canadian workforce. That's a message employers need to hear about.

Career practitioners and related service providers can contribute their voices in advocating for the stellar qualities these servicemen and servicewomen bring to civilian careers. **Challenge Factory**, for example, has done some first-rate work in this regard and has developed three resources targeted specifically to employer audiences.

1. *The Canadian Guide to Hiring Veterans* is an easy-to-use publication that helps employers find, hire, and retain military Veterans. It is free to download in PDF format and available for purchase in paperback. It offers:

   • Practical, reusable tools to make recruitment, hiring, and onboarding easier, including a hiring checklist, interview guide, onboarding framework, and more.

   • Myth-busting about Veterans in the workplace, through the use of relatable hiring scenarios, so it's clear why a Veteran should be an employer's next hire.

   • Evidence-based learning from Challenge Factory's research about the impact of using Veteran-hiring resources and how Veterans really act in civilian workplaces.

   • Resources compiled in one convenient place to help employers become Veteran friendly.

2. **MasterClass in Hiring** (https://www.centreforcareerinnovation.ca/courses/Hiring-Veterans-MasterClass) is an online course that equips employers with a roadmap for tapping into the hidden talent pool of Canada's Veterans.

   • Five learning modules build on the tips and lessons in *The Canadian Guide to Hiring Veterans*, a template for employers to create their own hiring action plan, and a course design that allows employers to choose their own learning path. The MasterClass focuses on shifting organizational culture and capacity, including career management learning, so that employers can find, hire, and retain quality hires.

- Employers who complete the MasterClass receive a Certificate of Completion, a Veteran Ready badge and toolkit for their marketing materials, and a listing on Challenge Factory's website of Veteran Ready Employers: https://www.centreforcareerinnovation.ca/pages/veteran-ready.

3. **The Glossary of Military to Civilian Career Transition Terms** (https://community.challengefactory.ca/dictionary/) provides clear definitions of terms used in military and career development contexts. By increasing access to essential terminology, the glossary helps everyone navigate the complexities of military language and better understand career transition.

Educating Educators and Trainers

Although many Canadian universities and community colleges offer Prior Learning Assessment and Recognition (PLAR),[60] each institution has a different set of rules in what they recognize. Their PLAR services are sometimes hard to locate, and what is offered does not shave much time off the requirements to obtain a degree or diploma.

Where then does that leave, for example, our newly transitioned Infantry Soldier who might be considering a new career path? Let's say she is successful in getting hired by a company to work in a job based solely on her military service record. Will her lack of civilian educational credentials impede upward mobility within that company? What if, after a few years with that company, she decides to seek employment elsewhere. Will the educational "shortfall" rear its head again? These questions get at some of the educational challenges an unprepared Veteran might encounter.

The Canadian Military, Veteran and Family Connected Campus Consortium (CMVF3C) [61] show significant promise in supporting military and Veteran communities. It aims to be a comprehensive resource hub for Veterans, military members, and their families, by providing a streamlined access to educational resources and opportunities. Through symposiums, training resources, consultations, and advocacy, the consortium is dedicated to addressing and easing the educational challenges faced by military members, Veterans, and their families as a result of their service. (See Chapter 12 for a list of participating institutions and what they offer).

Those military personnel with experience in **skilled trades** such as plumber, cook, automotive service technician, electrician, carpentry, welder, refrigeration, heavy-duty equipment operator, and more can apply to write provincial or territorial exams to receive Red Seal certification. More information on obtaining civilian credentials for military trades can be found at https://www.red-seal.ca/eng/others/dnd_2013_br.4ch.5r.2.shtml.

Before enlisting in further education or training, however, transitioning CAF members must determine what they want to do post-service and the qualifications needed to enter and practice in that career area. Not all occupations in the CAF naturally correspond to civilian roles, and even for those that do, the transitioning member may want to explore a career change. Not only can we help military members learn about careers but also about the civilian educational system, requirements for admission into colleges/universities or trade schools, and how to navigate within these spaces.

We can also share what we know about the military services and benefits for which they may be eligible. One noteworthy resource available to CAF Veterans is the Veterans Affairs Canada **Education Training Benefit** (ETB) that provides up to a maximum of $48,275 for Veterans who have served between 6 and 12 years and $96,550 for those serving 12 years and upwards.[62] This benefit can be used to help pay for tuition, course materials, living expenses, and other related training expenses. It is advisable to check the VAC website for updated funding amounts and to determine eligibility requirements.[63]

CAF Career Transition Services

Accessing the CAF's Career Transition Services should be top of mind for transitioning members way before leaving service. It sets them up for success by providing necessary information about the range of services and benefits available to facilitate a successful transition to civilian life and careers. As noted earlier, CAF Career Transition Services offers a number of services, including the following:

- **My Transition 101** – This training service provides information, support and tools needed to plan for life after military service. A second training unit is provided for members who are experiencing psychological/

mental health challenges and it incorporates lessons on identify, emotions and body/mind connections.

- **My Transition Seminars** – These seminars focus on preparing the member to understand the psychological impacts of transition as well as the financial and administrative readiness for release.

- **Transition Workshops** – Held on wings or bases across the country, these two-day workshops cover interest and skills assessment as well as interview and job-search techniques.

- **Long-Term Planning Seminars** – Topics include financial and budget planning, buying homes and understanding mortgages, wills and estate planning, pensions and benefits, and educational upgrading. CAF members are encouraged to participate within their first 10 years of service.

- **Individual Career or Educational Counselling** – One-on-one counselling is provided on topics like in-service transfers, educational upgrading, education reimbursement benefits, job-search assistance, and vocational rehabilitation recommendations.

VAC Career Transition Services

CAF Career Transition Services should ensure transitioning members are connected to Veterans Affairs Canada. There they will be able to access a range of rehabilitation and vocational assistance programs for Veterans to assist in achieving their career goals. A Veteran can take advantage of vocational rehabilitation programs that include assessment of one's abilities and aptitudes while considering education, training, experience, and the limitations of health challenges. Working with a Rehabilitation Specialist trained in vocational rehabilitation, the Veteran can explore achievable occupational goals as they learn to live with their injuries. Retraining and other job preparation services are also available and monitored with the help of a VAC Case Manager.

More Work to be Done

The Public Service Commission, Veterans Affairs Canada and other adjacent government organizations are mandated and/or committed to hiring a certain percentage of CAF Veterans and their spouses/partners. There is still more work to be done to engage small- to medium-sized private-sector companies in the business of hiring Veterans. In addition, consistent-across-the-board recognition criteria for prior learning, skills, and experience (which CMVF3C is in the process of developing) will definitely ease the military-to-civilian-education transition.

The National Veteran Employment Strategy's emphasis on building trusted partnerships includes post-secondary institutions. In time, this advocacy will likely yield rich results.

KEY LEARNING

★ Advocating for Veteran employment with employers must be an ongoing concern.

★ Several educational institutions across the country offer credit for military experience.

★ Provincial and territorial certification is available for those in the skilled trades.

★ CAF and VAC Career Transition Services have critical information that can help transitional members and Veterans in planning for employment as well as further education/training.

PART IV

The CAF as Employer

"Something I Always Wanted to Do"

At 12 years old, Alberto joined the cadets. Something about the order and structure attracted him. Because his family lived close to one of the CAF Air Force bases, he would always see the planes going through their maneuvers and dreamed of flying one day.

At 18, Alberto joined the CAF. Though the Air Force was his dream, the Navy was where people were needed at the time and that's where he served for six years before applying to the Air Force. Just shy of 39 years later, he retired as a Chief Warrant Officer, the highest rank in the non-commissioned member stream. (His wife also served for 36 years.)

Out since 2021, Alberto feels that the transition was planned and deliberate. "We knew we were getting toward that age," he reflects. "All the decisions we were making was trying to set ourselves up. Eight years before, we started planning. We attended a SCAN (Second Career Assistant Network) seminar, learned what we needed to be thinking about and looking at. We knew what we were going to be receiving for our pensions and that we would not need to seek for another job after we retired."

Prior to making the final decision, Alberto interviewed for a senior role in the CAF. "When you get to the level of Command Chief Warrant Officer, there aren't many other options to continue to serve." Thus, he and his wife decided in advance that if he weren't successful in getting that job, they would leave. And that's what they did when someone else was selected for the role.

Reconnecting with family and friends was one of the major goals after retirement. Now Alberto, together with his wife, does winter and summer fishing, plays hockey three times per week, runs frequently, plays golf, and serves on the board of directors of their golf club. As season ticket holders, they also enjoy watching their favourite Major Junior Hockey team. "We are chilling. Almost as busy as when we were in the military but now it's on our schedule."

Asked what he misses the most about life in the CAF, Alberto is emphatic: the people. "As you go through the military, you form a family with [y]our military friends, [as we did with] the ones we work closely with." Leaving them is hard but they keep in touch with those that are their friends.

He does not miss the busyness, the doing more with fewer people, the many and incessant meetings. His biggest adjustment to civilian life was the pace. He went from going, going all the time and travelling to being busy by choice in a very quiet place—away from the city, near to the water, surrounded by nature.

Alberto offers these gems of advice to those looking to transition out:

- ✓ "You don't want to do it on a whim. You want to be sure you are settled financially and know what you want to do. Plan it in advance."

- ✓ Know when it's time. I accepted to be a mentor on the Executive Leader Program after I officially retired and did that for two years. I felt I owed it to the institution and it was important to me to give a little bit back. After the two years was done, I felt that was enough. So know when it's time to finally leave.

- ✓ Be ready for things to take longer when you are out of the military. For example, when we were in uniform and were sick, we went to the Medical Inspection Room right away and were taken care of. Now it takes time to get a doctor and appointments.

Alberto expresses his thankfulness in being part of the Air Force's leadership team. For him it was a blessing. "I wanted to play a part and have an impact with the change of culture the Force was doing, as well as the importance of being inclusive."

But no regrets! "The opportunity I had to serve our great country was a great thing... so rewarding, and I'm so proud of our career."

CHAPTER 9

Recruiting, Onboarding, Benefits, and the Life

Based on 2021 Census data, 97,625 Canadians were counted as working for the Canadian Armed Forces.[64] It's indeed a large employer!

Occupations

Over 100 unique careers exist within the CAF, comprising Air Force, Army, and Navy, offering many opportunities to serve and see the world.[65] What is perhaps unexpected is the range of professional and skilled trade careers that one does not typically associate with the military—musicians, social workers, medical personnel, public affairs officers, physiotherapists, dentists, firefighters, police, skilled trades, pipers, chaplains, and pharmacists, to name a few.

Whatever one's level of education and training, from Grade 10 completion to university- and professional-degree qualifiers, the CAF provides opportunities to serve and work in full-time or part-time roles. One can join up to serve in the Regular Force or in the Reserve Force. Requirements differ based on the track one choses—officer track or non-commissioned members (NCM) track.

The CAF Value Proposition

Recognizing the distinct contributions made by those who serve Canada, the Canadian Armed Forces (CAF) Offer was established to ensure that all its members are appropriately recognized. This Offer includes a competitive set of benefits designed to attract new members and retain those who are currently serving.

- **Career Development**: The CAF Offer includes tools, training, and courses to help members develop their careers within the CAF. This element ensures that members have access to continuous professional development and growth opportunities.

- **Compensation**: The Compensation element provides competitive pay and supplemental allowances that increase as members advance in their military careers. This ensures that members are fairly compensated for their service and dedication.

- **Benefits**: The Benefits element encompasses a wide range of services, including medical, dental, injury, disability, educational, leave, and other service-related benefits. These benefits are designed to support the health and well-being of members and their families.

- **Work/Life Balance**: The My Work/Life element embodies a comprehensive wellness strategy that includes mental, spiritual, financial, physical, and overall well-being supports. This holistic approach aims to keep members and their families in top shape, ensuring they can balance their professional and personal lives effectively.

The Path to Becoming a CAF Member[66]

To join as a non-commissioned member, one must meet these minimum requirements:

- ✓ Be a Canadian citizen (or a permanent resident eligible to apply for Canadian citizenship) of good character

✓ Be 17 years of age (with parental consent) or older. Older applicants must be at an age to complete training and at least one term of service (3 years) prior to the mandatory retirement age of 60

✓ Have completed Grade 10 or 24 credits of Secondary IV (Quebec) or higher

✓ Be eligible to hold a security clearance

To join as an officer (commissioned member), one must:

✓ Be a Canadian citizen (or a permanent resident eligible to apply for Canadian citizenship) of good character

✓ Be 16 years of age (with parental consent) or older. Older applicants must be at an age to complete training and at least one term of service (3 years) prior to the mandatory retirement age of 60

✓ Have completed Grade 12 or Secondary V (Quebec) and have or be working toward a bachelor's degree

In addition, the applicant must possess an aptitude for learning; be motivated to serve in the CAF; exemplify values, attitudes, and characteristics befitting service in the CAF; and possess relevant skills.

Applicants can opt to serve in the Regular Force (full-time continuing), the Reserve Force (part-time non-continuing), or the Special Forces (full-time continuing when required by the Governor in Council). Interested candidates are encouraged to contact a recruiting centre (https://forces.ca/en/find-a-recruiting-centre/) to learn more about options, requirements, and exceptions.

Of note, there is a co-op option for high school students to become part of the CAF during the second semester of their school year.[67] Students can gain up to two high school credits by training with a CAF Army Reserve unit. During this Basic Training Co-op, which is conducted in Toronto, the student is out in the field for several days and has little or no contact with family, home, or friends while learning teamwork skills, first aid, military knowledge, and more. The program runs from February to June. After completing the co-op, the student can apply to continue with the CAF and complete their trade-level training and/or take the offer of full-time summer employment.

To be eligible for the high school co-op, one must:

- ✓ Be a Canadian citizen
- ✓ Have completed a minimum of 15 secondary school credits
- ✓ Be 17 by the beginning of Semester 2
- ✓ Have a clean criminal record
- ✓ Be medically fit
- ✓ Have had no involvement with illegal substance in the 6 months prior to their application

Is This for Me?

- If the thought of committing to full-time military service in the Regular Force is daunting, the Reserves offers the same opportunity to serve while going to school full-time or working full-time in the civilian world. While a member of the Reserves, one can apply to serve full-time for a term. Note that The Reserve Employment Opportunities website (https://mcsportal-portaillcm.forces.gc.ca/REO/en/index.aspx) lists currently available positions within the Reserve Force specifically.

  - ○ The Navy offers a Naval Experience Program (NEP) where one can get exposure to life in the Navy for one year before committing to service.[68]

Securing a Career in the CAF

There are five steps to securing a career in the CAF.

1. **Application** – Documents to be submitted include birth certificate, photo ID, educational transcripts, trade qualifications, and/or licences and any other documents required for the career area selected. If education was obtained outside of Canada, a Canadian equivalency must be assessed through Alliance of Credential Evaluation Services of Canada (https://canalliance.org/en/).

2. **Reliability Screening** – This involves filling out reliability screening forms to ensure the applicant can be trusted with sensitive information. The CAF will verify all forms submitted for honesty.

3. **Aptitude and Personality Assessment** – There is an aptitude test to help determine which military job the applicant is best suited for, though a trial currently underway affects when the test is taken and how the results are used.[69] Non-commissioned members who have completed a degree (or equivalent), completed a college diploma on the Military Occupation list, meet the ideal entry-level requirement of one's target occupation, or meet an employment application form score are eligible for the trial. The test is one hour long and evaluates verbal skills, spatial ability, and problem-solving abilities at the high school level. In addition, a personality inventory is included.

4. **Medical Examination** – This will take place in two parts. Part 1 is completion of a questionnaire on the applicant's medical history inclusive of current medications, followed by a physical examination to determine height, weight, vision, colour perception, and hearing. Part 2 is a review of applicant's medical file to determine if any limitations are present that will impact training or career.

5. **Interview** – Conducted by a military career counsellor, the interview constitutes the applicant's official job interview. Questions will be asked about employment history, knowledge of the CAF, and understanding of the job for which the candidate is applying. The interview is used to determine a person's fit for both job and the ideal work environment.

Basic Training

After being accepted by the CAF, all personnel must undergo basic training at the Canadian Forces Leadership and Recruit School in Quebec. This nine-week Basic Military Officer Qualification (BMQ) is designed to build teamwork skills, physical fitness, what constitutes professional conduct, and core military skills. The physical fitness component comprises sandbag lifts; sandbag drags, 20-metre rushes, and intermittent load shuttles. A typical training day starts at 5 am, ends between 6 and 7 pm, and is followed by 2 to 3 hours of evening preparations for the next day.

Salary and Benefits

Consistent with its value proposition referenced earlier, the CAF offers competitive salaries. Starting salaries are aligned with equivalent entry-level careers in the private sector. A new direct entry recruit in the Regular Force can earn anywhere from $3,614 to $5,304 per month.[70] Members' salaries are based on their pay group, rank, and years of service. (Note: This opens up another area in which the Veteran may need assistance from us. Because they never had to negotiate their salaries, since these are on a set scale, they may not know how to do this when they transition to the private sector. In fact, they may not even be aware this is a critical skill to have and to use.)

Specialty pay is available within certain occupational roles.

Benefits include four weeks of annual vacation to start and several paid educational programs. There are four main categories by which military members can receive paid or subsidized education:[71]

1. **Non-Commissioned Member Subsidized Training Plan (NCMSTEP)** – Provides full-time paid training for studies related to military jobs. This program is open to all non-commissioned members (not officers)—sailors, soldiers, and aviators.

2. **Regular Officer Training Plan (ROTP)** – Through this program, one can obtain an officer commission as well as an undergraduate degree. Degrees can be obtained at the Canadian Military College or at another Canadian university. Officers are leaders, planners, policymakers, and managers and must hold a university degree.

3. **Indigenous Leadership Opportunity Year** – This one-year prep education program is open to Indigenous people in Canada through the Royal Military College in Kingston, Ontario. After successful completion, the individual can apply to the Royal Military College in a degree program.

4. **Specialty Programs** at the graduate and undergraduate level are available. Medical Officer Training is for those wanting to be doctors, Dental Officer Training for aspiring dentists, and Nursing/Pharmacy Training for future pharmacists and nurses. In addition, **Subsidized Education for Entry Level Masters (SEELM)** is available for aspiring physiotherapists, social workers, and chaplains wishing to serve thus in the CAF.

Note: After graduation from a paid educational program, a job is guaranteed in one's field of study within the CAF. Two months of service is required for every month of paid education.

As career practitioners, we are always on the lookout for employment opportunities to recommend to our clients. And when a client's assessment results show that they value working in a structured, stable environment that also provides job security, a career in the CAF may just be the perfect option, especially if the client's interests and personality also align with that work environment.

★ A variety of careers exist within the CAF, including some unexpected ones.

★ A Grade 10 education is the minimum educational requirement needed.

★ Basic training will test one's physical and mental fitness.

★ There are ways to try out military service before committing.

★ Paid education and training is available through the CAF, but service is required to offset it.

YVONNE'S FAVOURITES

◎ The **Canadian Armed Forces Education-Experience-Equivalency (CAF 3E)** (https://caface-rfacace.forces.gc.ca/en/index) allows anyone wishing to join the military to discover what credit/recognition they can receive for previous education and experience.

PART V

Career Needs of Military Spouses/ Partners

"Our family transitioned four times in five years. I was always starting over."

—Elaine Piper

"Community, Communication, Respect"

Simone holds a master's degree in adult education and has been a military spouse for 10 years. Prior to her husband's decision to join, Simone says her perspective of the military was ambivalent at best. Not being comfortable with aggressive warfare, she wondered about the kind of people she would meet and be associated with.

Before starting their family, she had made the decision that she would be a stay-at-home mom. She completed her M.Ed. around the same time her first child was born. Work outside the home consisted of projects and causes she believed in and was passionate about. She worked in non-profit as well as in fibre arts, volunteered, and taught adult education on evenings and weekends. She loved the work she was doing, and when the option was on the table to consider a career in the military for her husband, her patchwork career was already her lived reality by choice.

She recalls many discussions with her husband prior to his joining. By then, their two children were 7 and 9 years old. Her husband made it clear that if it was not something she wanted their family to do, she should just tell him no. She really appreciated that!

The family relocated from the west coast to the east and moved into military housing. The base was right next door to their home, which allowed Simone to contribute through volunteering and to also readily access services. Though she did not have a language barrier, still, it was a big adjustment. Her oldest child admits that it was a very hard adjustment for her at the time. They stayed in military housing for seven years.

After three years as a military spouse, Simone decided to look for full-time employment and secured a contract with the federal government. When her husband was deployed for the first time, she opted to work part-time and got a job as a bank teller. Between these roles and volunteering she admits that her career progression took a small hit. How do you explain these multiple roles didn't fit into a cohesive career trajectory? "I think a lot of military spouses come with so much training, intelligence, and abilities and things they can offer but a lot of them are underestimated. Employers seem to believe that because they have had these odd jobs, that they are less intelligent."

For the last five years, Simone has been a public servant. "One of the reasons I chose work with the public service is that I had in the back of my mind that if we had to relocate, at least I have a 'leg up' by my choosing to pursue work in the government instead of starting over from scratch."

Unlike other families, they have not moved. Although her husband has been offered postings elsewhere, they have advocated to maintain stability for their family. Simone admits that the last couple of years have been rough for her family and she's grateful they were close to needed resources within the community during that period. She's confident, however, that had they needed to move, they would have survived.

Over the years, Simone has come to appreciate the role the military plays, how pivotal it is in crisis intervention and how overstretched it is. She recognizes the sacrifice and dedication it takes for someone to choose this life, the fact that so much has changed in the world over the last 10 years, and how the need for serving members surpasses the military's capacities. All these factors have shifted her attitude from ambivalence to greater appreciation.

Then there is the sense of cohesion, helpfulness, and collaboration from serving members and families. "When our kids were younger, any time I needed something, someone would immediately step up. When a deployment happens, you literally just put a message out there in the community chat, and someone will get milk for your baby, or boost your car battery."

On the down side, Simone feels that military life, especially frequent postings, results in some families being yanked around the country with little thought given to the consequences for supporting partners and children, who can feel like pawns sometimes. The military machine does not always factor in how hard these moves are on spouses and kids. For example, kids may have special needs. and now they have to move to a new community where the necessary supports may not exist, the family cannot afford housing, military housing is not available, etc. Sometimes spouses and children have to stay behind.

Simone does not think her career development has been significantly impacted by their family's choice to serve. She admits that not being posted and being able to say no to some postings helped a lot. However, "by and large, I feel like I've gotten where I am mostly on my own ability and experience and mindset." She feels she had the primary ingredients already in place for doing well as a military spouse—resilience, taking charge of her own life, and having no difficulty asking for help.

She shares this advice:

- ✓ Don't be afraid to ask for help. The resources available are very helpful. Definitely access them and use them. That's what they are there for.

- ✓ On your CV, talk not just about your skills or your jobs, but highlight your openness, adaptability, willingness to learn, and ability to pivot.

- ✓ To the serving spouse/partner she says, "Open communication lines with your partner is really key. If these are solid and clear there is lots less disappointment. Discuss the impact of each move on the family." Having the support from the military member is crucial to the person left behind. Everyone has a stake in each move. Respect each other and communicate.

- ✓ To public service employers she says, "PSC [the Public Service Commission] can put the same priority on spouses that they put on hiring Veterans. They may not have the medals to show for it but they too have done their part."

CHAPTER 10

Understanding the Needs of Military Spouses and Families

Those who serve in occupations to defend and protect our personal and civil liberties strongly benefit from the support of family, mentors, peer networks, and service providers. What, though, do we know of the family members, particularly the civilian or non-serving spouses, who serve at home while their loved one is serving their country?

Realities of Life for the Military Family

Back in 2013, CAF Ombudsman Pierre Daigle tendered a special report to the Minister of National Defence.[72] This report examined how well the families of today's Canadian Armed Forces were doing. As a preamble to the findings of the report, Daigle provided some important contextual points:

- Canada has been engaged in more complex and challenging missions since 1990.

- The duration and challenges of these types of military engagements have taken a toll on families.

- There has been an increase in the number of family-related complaints to the DND and the CAF.

The research focused on the families of 370 current and recently retired CAF members. Overall findings indicated that families (1) were proud of their contributions to making their family situations work in spite of the challenges of having a parent or partner on active military duty; and (2) value some of the benefits of military family life, such as more bilingual educational opportunities for their children and the ability to live in different locations. The research also revealed, however, that relocation and deployments cause major disruption and put strain on families.

Enter Seamless Canada. Supporting the employment needs of military families has become one of Canada's priorities, and Seamless Canada was launched by the DND and CAF in 2018 to improve services to CAF members and families when they relocate to a different province or territory. This includes easing access to provincial and territorial employment, health care, and child care resources that can be used before and during relocation. On the Seamless Canada web page,[73] one can simply select the province or territory they will be moving to and immediately access Military Family Resource Centres in that province, spouse/partner employment resources, as well as education, child care, and health care services.

While the above are much-needed to address the challenges of military life, that life is what it is. And the following realities are constants in the lives of every military family:

1. **Mobility**: relocation on average every three to five years within Canada or abroad and over which they have little or no input/influence

2. **Separation**: ongoing or periodic separation associated with deployments and training

3. **Risk**: living with the inherent dangers associated with military training and service

One could argue that these realities are not unique to military families. It's true—they aren't. But while many other professions include one or more of these challenges, very few demand *all three*. With regards to separation and risk, while the serving partner is working long hours, deployed, or on training, the military spouse is the one responsible for keeping the family unit afloat and functioning smoothly. On average, military families relocate three times more often than the average Canadian family,[74] which can contribute to further strain on the spouse. All three realities combined often contribute to a less-than-conventional career path for the civilian military spouse.

The rest of this chapter will focus on military spouses/partners: how their career development and employment prospects are impacted by the military lifestyle, and how career practitioners can help them mitigate some of their common employment challenges.

The Military Spouse: Characteristics and Statistics

The profile of a military spouse includes some or all of these characteristics:

- Military spouses are a talented group of individuals. Due to the nature of the military lifestyle, spouses develop qualities and skills highly valued by employees: problem solving, flexibility, adaptability, critical thinking, organization, resiliency, project management, creativity, and leadership.

- Military spouses frequently experience challenges in finding employment and building their careers, resulting in unemployment or underemployment.

- Frequent relocations can limit continuing education opportunities and make it difficult for a spouse to accrue seniority at work.

- When opportunity is scarce, especially in remote military communities, military spouses often settle for jobs that are below their skill level and education, thus limiting their own professional growth and development.

- Military spouses demonstrate incredible resourcefulness by seeking continuing education and/or volunteer experiences when employment opportunities are not available.

- Female military spouses are significantly more likely to have lower employment income after a residential move than those who have not relocated.[75]

We also know a few things about the education and credentials of military spouses:[76]

- 62% of military spouses have a post-secondary education, making them a highly educated group.

- 25% of military spouses work in a regulated profession, but despite the existence of pan-Canadian Labour Mobility provisions, military spouses still come up against credential recognition and licensure barriers when looking for work in their chosen profession.

Research on Military and Veteran Families

Pierre Daigle's report also noted the following:[77]

- Military families have little control over the location, timing, or duration of relocations.

- Most families noted that it could take from a month to as long as a year for them to shift back into their regular family rhythm after a deployment and that this has a significant impact on partner and children relationships.

- The majority of partners experienced unemployment or underemployment challenges since becoming military spouses, especially when posted in small communities where there are even fewer employment options.

- The majority of non-serving partners expressed frustration at being the one to make all the professional sacrifices required once children are brought into the union.

In a review of over 100 reports from 2008 to 2018 regarding military families, Lynda Manser identified the following data:[78]

- Of the 66,000 Regular Force members, 50% reported being in a legal relationship and/or parents.

- Nearly 4,000 Regular Force members are single parents.

- One-third of Regular Force members and their families posted in Canada live in the vicinity of Ottawa, Halifax, and Valcartier.

- Most commonly cited challenges facing Canadian military families include issues with personal well-being and mental health, financial stress, and relationship strain.

- Canadian research suggests that 80% of military families are resilient and feel supported within the CAF community; further, 90% felt that they were successfully meeting the responsibilities of their family lives, and 10% felt otherwise.

- Many families do not avail themselves of the resources provided through their Military Resources Centres, but those who did were satisfied with the services they received and believed they were beneficial.

* * *

What all of these statistics tell us is that CAF military spouses are educated, adaptable, mobile, diverse, and in the prime of life. Their career development and employment prospects, however, are impacted by the military lifestyle. In the next chapter, we will see how they can tap into their many positive characteristics to overcome some of the employment challenges they face.

KEY LEARNING

★ The life of a military family is disrupted more often than that of most civilian families.

★ Military spouses are diverse, educated, hard-working, and adaptable.

★ Most families are proud of the contributions they make on behalf of their families to support the serving member and their country.

★ Many military families do not access the full range of resources provided.

CHAPTER 11

Military Spouses – Overcoming Employment Challenges

Military spouses as a group face a number of employment challenges: difficulty in developing their careers or finding and sustaining employment; being overlooked for promotions due to inconsistent or short-term employment history; inability to accrue seniority due to frequent relocations; having their career development or professional training impeded based on location; limited employment prospects when posted in small or rural communities. Such challenges not only affect spouses' career development, they also impact the financial stability of their families.

Relocation lies at the root of most of the challenges listed above. From a report by Lynda Manser on this topic,[79] we learn the following about military spouses:

- 37% of spouses felt they had to take a job for which they were overqualified because of having to relocate.

- Finding employment that matched their education and experience was the biggest challenge of relocations.

- Relocations often added extra strain on partner/spousal relationships.

- From an infographic synthesis of the 2018 report *State of Military Families in Canada*,[80] we also learn that 50% of respondents felt that their financial situations became worse after a relocation due to decrease in income of the non-military spouse, higher housing costs, and higher cost of living in the new location.

Programs and Resources

How then do we help the military spouse whose opportunity to earn a living is severely impacted by the military lifestyle? Let's look at a few programs.

Military Spouse Employment Initiative (MSEI)

https://www.canada.ca/en/department-national-defence/corporate/job-opportunities/civilian-jobs/civilian-job-opportunities/military-spouse-employment-initiative.html

MSEI provides tools and resources for military spouses and partners to not only develop skills but also pursue careers within the federal Public Service through inventories, employment pools, and other government staffing programs.

From the inventory of jobs within the Canadian Public Service, spouses can access opportunities in many areas, including the following:

- Information technology
- General labour
- Trades
- Health care
- Engineering
- Communications and public relations
- Office administration
- Human resources
- Teaching/education
- Procurement services

- Social sciences

- Food services

- Cleaning services

Simone, one of the military spouses profiled in the guide, says, "One of the reasons I chose work with the public service is that I had in the back of my mind that if we had to relocate, at least I have a 'leg up' by my choosing to pursue work in the government instead of starting over from scratch." So yes, while relocation is a reality, spouses can access a range of employment opportunities within the government of Canada. And also, now that remote work is more widely accepted, relocations do not always have to mean losing a job and having to find a new one.

Military Spousal Employment Network (MSEN)

https://msen.vfairs.com/en

MSEN is an online hub that is exclusive to military spouse and partners to build connections with employer partners and empower careers. Through the MSEN, spouses can explore a national list of employers and connect with hiring managers. Members can see available job openings, participate in career fairs, post resumes, and build their professional network. Being online, it can be accessed from anywhere and is particularly relevant for spouses who are overseas and looking to return to work in Canada.

Canadian Forces Morale and Welfare Services (CFMWS)

https://cfmws.ca/

Provides programs and services for CAF members, Veterans, their families across Canada and overseas in a variety of domains, including financial literacy and resiliency (SISIP Financial), relocation, family transition support, and more. Great resources for military spouses are as follows:

CareerCOACH+

https://cfmws.ca/careercoach

- Free, virtual, and confidential career coaching, connecting military spouses/partners directly to a professional career coach for tailored support with career transition, development, and employment pursuits.

- Military spouses can access support for up to five one-hour sessions.

Virtual group career development training

https://cfmws.ca/support-services/employment/career-development

- Free career development education and training specifically tailored for military spouses, covering topics such as quantifying your resumé, negotiating tactics, creating LinkedIn content, constructing a professional profile statement, increasing networking skills, etc.
- Helping Entrepreneurs Reach Complete Success (HERCS) and a Portfolio Development Program are also available.

Second language training

https://cfmws.ca/support-services/education/second-language-training

- Second Language Training learning resources and tools allow users to increase their language skills and may help them integrate into a new community, add a new language skill to their resumé, or prepare for a posting outside of Canada.

Family Information Line

https://cfmws.ca/support-services/family-information-line

1-800-866-4546 (North America) / 00-800-771-17722 (International)

- This is a confidential, personal, bilingual, and free service offering information, support, referrals, reassurance, and crisis management to the military community.

Professional Licences and Accreditation

One of the difficulties experienced as a result of relocations is differing provincial standards for practice. The Labour Mobility provisions of the Canadian Free Trade Agreement (https://workersmobility.ca/) allow certified workers to be recognized as qualified to work in another province or territory as long as that recognition comes from a body that regulates that occupation. No additional training, exams, or assessments will be required unless an exception has been posted.

The challenge is that under the current framework, provinces can post exceptions to particular trades or occupational groups, thereby overriding the spirit of the Agreement. At the time of this writing, five provinces (Ontario, Alberta,

Saskatchewan, Nova Scotia, Newfoundland and Labrador) had exceptions in place affecting a number of occupational groups (dental hygienists, denturists, drinking water system operators, lawyers, licensed practical nurses, medical radiation technologists, midwives, nurse practitioners, paramedics, podiatrists, psychologists, safety code officers, social workers, water well drillers).

This is a good example of how problematic and frustrating licensure can be for a military spouse/partner who may be employed in one of the identified groups and who may be required to move across provinces every two to three years. That said, each province has a Labour Mobility Coordinator so it is advisable to contact each prior to moving.

Taking Control

Spouses can take proactive steps to limit the need to restart their career every time they move. Career practitioners can encourage spouses to think outside the box and strategically explore careers that have the possibility to sustain them throughout military life and afterwards. They can invest in:

- Building their social networks
- Exploring remote work options
- Maintaining an accomplishment portfolio
- Volunteering to build skills
- Seeking employment with CFMWS, located in military communities, and with Outside of Canada (OUTCAN) possibilities (https://cfmws.ca/about-us/cfmws-careers)
- Taking courses and accessing online learning to enhance credentials
- Entrepreneurship
- Turning a hobby into an income generator online
- Writing a book, creating a podcast, and so much more.

Elaine Piper recommends doing an online business, adopting an entrepreneurial mindset, or exploring what services spouses can offer virtually, especially if they are a subject matter expert in what they do.

These are great ideas, but the truth of the matter is, sometimes the jobs our clients desire are just not available. When this happens, and after they've come to terms with the reality, we can often nudge them in a new direction.

✓ Invite clients to work differently, and to see work differently. Does it always have to be done in its traditional setting?

✓ Help clients to leverage technology and social media to create opportunities. If your client used to teach or counsel and there are no local jobs, could he do online teaching, tutoring, or counselling?

✓ Encourage clients to ask for what they need. One spouse, on receiving the news that her family was about to be relocated, did just that. She presented a case to her employer that demonstrated how she could continue to do the same job working from home. She anticipated and addressed all the employer's concerns as well as how her solution would save the employer money. Her request was granted and she even received a promotion while working from home.

A change of perspective is sometimes all that is required to get our clients moving in a new direction.

Remote Career Options

Let's take a look at remote or hybrid careers. We can help spouses who are tired of the hassle of having to worry about getting a job every time they relocate by encouraging them to explore what I have dubbed "beyond borders" careers. A quick search on Indeed for Remote work in Halifax, Nova Scotia (for example), yielded the following roles:

- Medical scribe
- Solution specialist
- Designer
- Communication advisor
- Customer service representative
- Talent strategist
- Freight broker
- Risk analyst
- Instructional designer

- Marketing specialist

- Nurse

- Broker

- Psychologist

The COVID-19 pandemic showed us that work could happen in places and spaces that we heretofore thought impossible. All of us career practitioners can recall how we had to quickly pivot and come up with creative ways to offer services. I personally have not returned to working in an office building and, for activities that I thought could only work with clients in person, I have invented new, and may I say better, ways to connect with clients.

Of course, there are certain things best done in person, but effective work can be done and done well working remotely. When homes become offices, when workers have the flexibility to be accountable for getting the job done when no one is watching, and when employers want to save on expensive office buildings to house said workers, military spouses can fit the bill. Their resilience, flexibility, commitment, and perseverance despite challenges make them excellent candidates for remote work. And as the Indeed search above illustrates, the range of jobs that can be done remotely is wide.

Addressing Employer Biases in the Interview

We have already documented the many skills that military spouses posses as a direct result of living the military lifestyle: adaptability, flexibility, problem solving, creativity, and so on. The key for spouses is to recognize these skills in themselves and know how to communicate them to a prospective employer.

For the military spouse wishing to pursue traditional employment, the key to success is preparation. For example, how do we equip spouses to address these four questions/concerns employers might have:

1. Why have you had so many employment changes and/or jobs not related to your education or training?

2. Why do you have so many volunteer or continuing education experiences?

3. Why is your resumé in a functional, not chronological, format?

4. Why should I bother hiring you? You'll be gone in a few months.

Using elements of hope-centred coaching, we can help military spouses prepare responses to address such questions. Let's do so now for a fictional client, Céleste Augustine. You'll find her resumé in Appendix 2. Notice that Céleste has gaps in her employment experience and that she has held positions for short periods of time. Céleste's resumé illustrates how the military lifestyle can impact a military spouse's employment history. (And yes, here as well as in Mason Cummings's resumé, there are a few minor fixes that I will leave for you to spot.)

Employer bias #1: When reviewing the resume of a military spouse who has held many short-term jobs, jobs unrelated to education or training, or jobs that are entry-level in nature, an employer might assume that the candidate is unambitious, lazy, an underperformer, or unreliable.

Addressing employer bias #1: Through practice interviews, career practitioners can teach clients how to communicate the reason for the seeming deficits while keeping the focus on the fact that, despite the challenges, they were able to acquire skills. A possible answer for someone like Céleste might be: "Every move means searching for a new job. I have to conduct market research to determine what opportunities are available in my new community, network with people who can provide information needed, step out of my comfort zone, and do what needs to be done to advance both my own career development and meet my family's financial needs. Sometimes the work that is available is different from what I was trained to do, offers lower compensation or is contractual in nature. In every one of these jobs, I ensured I was a major contributor to the organization. My previous employers will all attest to my reliability, responsibility, and strong work ethic."

Employer bias #2: A resumé that shows a higher-than-normal amount of volunteer or continuing-education experience may cause an employer to wonder if the spouse is seriously interested in working.

Addressing employer bias #2: While this is not the case for Céleste, a possible answer could be: "In many of the locations where my spouse was posted there were no jobs to be found. Because I have created a strategic plan for building my career, I determined that in situations where I could not find paid employment I would instead seek out specific volunteer or educational opportunities that would help me develop skills in line with my strategic plan. I believe in being resourceful and maximizing the opportunities at my disposal rather than bemoaning things I cannot change." What employer would not be impressed!

Employer bias #3: A candidate who has submitted a functional rather than a chronological resumé must be hiding something.

Addressing employer bias #3: A possible answer could be: "I have chosen a non-chronological resumé format to showcase my experiences. Every work opportunity I had taught me something different. The tasks may have been the same, but the way I work or the people I have worked with meant that I needed to consistently modify my approach or methods to get the job done. I wanted to communicate the broad range of skills I have that can help an organization meet its goals. Longevity in a job does not necessarily mean that a person is being effective. I know how to work hard. I am a creative problem-solver, have had to project-manage all our moves and apply critical-thinking skills to every new posting challenge. These are the qualities I can bring to this job."

Employer bias #4: Military families are always on the move. It does not make sense to hire a military spouse or invest in their training. They will be gone before I can reap the benefits of my investment.

Addressing employer bias #4: The reality is that the average duration of a military posting is anywhere from three to five years (this may vary based on circumstances).[81] So even though mobility is a characteristic of military life, the frequency of moves does not affect all military members to the same degree. And as stated earlier, remote work is here to stay. This opens up a wealth of possibilities for military spouses whose flexibility, commitment, and solution-focused thinking gets the job done, no matter where they are located.

Hopefully, these sample responses illustrate the role military spouses can play in shaping their own career destinies and how we can guide them in addressing employer biases.

Advocating for and with Military Spouses

Career practitioners can coach military spouses/partners on techniques to advocate for themselves and teach them to look at their experiences through strength-based lenses. Their adaptability, resilience, and courage should not be taken for granted by them or anyone else. And it goes without saying that raising employer awareness about the spousal component of the military lifestyle and its impact on career development will help mitigate the biases and misconceptions. By so doing, an enlightened employer can focus on the candidate's strengths rather than their history, and suspend judgement about the reason for a candidate's perceived deficits.

Almost a decade old, the following recommendations for career practitioners working with military spouses from Katie Ochin, former Employment and Entrepreneurship Program Manager with Military Family Services, remain relevant:

- Military spouses are resilient, adaptable, and strong, but they may need assistance demonstrating these strengths in their employment applications. Taking them through a skills inventory exercise may be effective.

- Encourage military spouses to explore mobile employment and remote working opportunities.

- Encourage military spouses to take advantage of online training and development opportunities.

- Review military spouses' answers to key interview questions and work together to decide how an unorthodox employment history can be addressed in a strength-based way.

- Teach military spouses how to advocate for themselves and the skills they bring to the job market.

Despite the stresses and challenges of relocation, military spouses are interested in finding personal fulfillment, maintaining their skills and career status, and gaining independence. They are motivated to work and know how to work hard. They have been doing it for a long time.

A Plethora of Support

There exists a vast support system for military spouses/partners and families. Below are the critical gateways to these supports:

Military Family Services (MFS)

https://cfmws.ca/support-services/families

MFS, a division of CFMWS, recognizes the important role families have in enabling the operational readiness of the Canadian Armed Forces. From toolkits to partnerships, MFS offers programming and support to CAF family members in a variety of areas, such as relocation, caregiving, deployment, healthy relationships, bereavement and grief, children and youth, etc. This includes access to skilled professionals, networking opportunities, employment training, and other services designed to support their needs. Visit the MFS website for full details.

Military Family Resource Centres (MFRC)

https://cfmws.ca/support-services/families/
military-family-resource-centres

- MFRCs are essentially the heart of their military communities. Staff members are dedicated front-line service providers, responsible for connecting military families to a wide range of programs and services. You'll be invited to ask questions about parenting or employment, volunteer in meaningful ways, make new friends, connect with old friends, or learn new skills.

- Here you can find the location and contact information for each of the Military Family Resource Centres in Canada as well as the programs and services offered.

KEY LEARNING

★ Military spouses face unique employment challenges.

★ Military Spouse Employment Initiative (MSEI) and Military Spousal Employment Network (MSEN) are key employment programs for military spouses/partners.

★ With proper coaching, and by tapping into areas of strength, employer concerns and misconceptions can be addressed.

★ Family and other supports are critical to helping military members transition. Military Family Services can help.

◎ **Military Spousal Employment Network (MSEN)** (https://msen.vfairs.com/en). Online and exclusive to military spouses and partners, MSEN is a great resource to access a range of employment related services.

"Wherever Life Plants You, Choose to Grow"

Choosing to grow is what Dahlia lived for the 26 years that she's been a military spouse. All she knew about military life in advance was a vague idea that it would include moving. "I honestly didn't have any perception about the military lifestyle!" One of her biggest challenges was to be away from family, so Dahlia chose to make friends everywhere they moved. For her, the social aspect was, and still is, important.

She admits that in the early years she didn't really deal well with the many changes their family had to make. Her husband was away a lot and most of the family responsibilities fell on her. It was a mental load. However, with time and experience she's learned to organize and change her attitude. Instead of stressing unduly and bemoaning what is, she kept herself in a state of readiness, choosing to grow wherever she was and despite the circumstances.

To this day, Dahlia still finds it exciting to move to a new city, province, or country. She loves learning about new cultures and ways of life whether she's living in Canada or overseas. "Every time, we had great experiences and made good friends." On the flip side however, it was difficult to leave these friends behind and constantly having to find a new job. Posting messages would always come late and there was little time to search for a job in advance because there was so much else to do, like buying a house, settling in, finding a new school, a new dentist, a new doctor, and more.

"Twenty-six years ago," Dahlia reflects, "there were no services like today to support military spouses. Prior to having kids, I had low-paying jobs because we were moving every two years. When the kids were born, we couldn't find a daycare so we decided that I would stay home. Once the kids were in school, I was able to go back to work. Back in those days, when you were applying on a job, you couldn't mention that you were a military spouse because chances are, you wouldn't get the position. I lost a few jobs because I was honest, and explained why I moved so many times."

Dahlia says that in all of her career she's never been paid more than $25 per hour, despite having an undergraduate degree. At their current location, being francophone and lacking confidence in her English-language skills is a major disadvantage to finding work, so she is still unemployed and looking for a full-time job.

Her best advice to new military spouses/partners is to ensure that they have a transportable career. However if that is not the case, she suggests the following for consideration:

- ✓ Build a solid resumé with great transferable skills. Take the Portfolio sessions [MFS Portfolio Development Program].
- ✓ Consider going back to school or take courses that can help you get a better job.
- ✓ Know yourself and make sure that what you do brings you joy. This will have a big impact on your relationship with your spouse and the people around you.
- ✓ Learn a new language (become bilingual).
- ✓ Start your own business.
- ✓ Inform yourself on how CFMWS and MFS Employment can help you with your career.
- ✓ Don't be shy to seek help.

Dahlia adds that while military life is not always easy on the spouse's career, she firmly believes that we are responsible for our choices. "I maybe didn't prepare myself enough, and if I could go back, I would change a thing or two. I am grateful for my life and experiences and my advice for future military spouses is to be aware of what you are getting yourself into. Have the conversation concerning your career goals and how you can attain them in parallel with your husband's career."

When they eventually leave military service, Dahlia wants to settle close to family and finally focus on her career.

Programs and Resources

CHAPTER 12

Services, Programs, and Resources

Here you will find a list of Canadian military and civilian service providers and areas of specialty in six categories. Please bear in mind that this list is neither comprehensive nor exhaustive. Organizations that are doing great work on behalf of CAF members and Veterans might have been missed.

In each category, organizations and resources that are critical as starting points are listed first and starred (*); the rest are in alphabetical order.

Employment

This list comprises organizations or resources that are dedicated to helping transitioning and Veteran CAF members prepare for, and secure, employment.

Digital Transition Centre*

https://www.canada.ca/en/department-national-defence/services/benefits-military/transition.html

This includes virtual access to transition counselling, electronic release administration, access to transition training and education initiatives. Within the DTC, there is also My Skills and Education Translator (My SET), which is continuing to evolve and helps equate some military skills and experiences with civilian academic credentials. In addition, there is the MNET, which helps to equate military occupations with their civilian counterparts.

Military Transition Engagement & Partnerships (MTEP)*

https://www.canada.ca/en/department-national-defence/services/benefits-military/transition/mtep.html

A digital national network for organizations, businesses, and programs that support transitioning military/Veterans and their families. Organizations or service providers supportive of the military, Veteran, and family communities can join by going to the MTEP landing page and submitting a registration form to become part of the National Resource Directory (NRD). Once in the NRD, organizations will also be able to share best practices in supporting these populations.

CAF Career Transition Services*

https://www.canada.ca/en/department-national-defence/services/benefits-military/transition/caf-career-transition-services.html

Provides assistance with second careers, career transition workshops, a vocational program for serving members, referral to sources of employment within the federal Public Service, toolkits, and more.

BMO Canada

https://jobs.bmo.com/ca/en/military

As the official bank of the Canadian Defence community, BMO offers career opportunities for CAF service personnel, Veterans, and their families. In addition to career opportunities, BMO Canada offers financial literacy tips for Veterans, an entrepreneurship guide, military leave top-up benefits, discounted bank service fees, and more.

Canadian Corps of Commissionaires

https://www.commissionaires.ca

This is a private, not-for-profit Canadian company employing over 20,000 people in security or protective positions across the country. For businesses, they provide security guard services, security consultation, investigations, and para-policing services. For individuals, they offer fingerprinting services, criminal record checks, record suspensions and pardons, and USA entry waivers, protection, and more. The Canadian Corps of Commissionaires is one of the largest employers of Canadian vets.

The Canadian Guide to Hiring Veterans

https://www.challengefactory.ca/VeteranHiringGuide

An easy-to-use publication that helps employers find, hire, and retain military Veterans. It is free to download in PDF format and available for purchase in paperback. It offers:

- Practical, reusable tools to make recruitment, hiring, and onboarding easier, including a hiring checklist, interview guide, onboarding framework, and more.

- Myth-busting about Veterans in the workplace, through the use of relatable hiring scenarios, so it's clear why a Veteran should be an employer's next hire.

- Evidence-based learning from Challenge Factory's research about the impact of using Veteran-hiring resources and how Veterans really act in civilian workplaces.

- Resources compiled in one convenient place to help employers become Veteran friendly.

COPSystem

https://www.edits.net/via

Provides a full assessment of interests, abilities, and work values. Occupations that match all three areas are flagged in gold, and occupations that match two areas are noted in silver. Though American and connected to the Occupational Information Network (O*NET), this assessment tool does provide a National Occupational Classification (NOC) document that can be downloaded at https://copsystem.edits.net/public/ccg-c-wbb.pdf.

Education and Training Benefit

https://veterans.gc.ca/en/education-and-jobs/go-back-school/education-and-training-benefit

This is funding specifically geared to military members looking to go back to school or upgrade their education including shorter courses, business boot camps, workshops, and seminars. Members are able to apply until 10 years after their release date.

Employers Seeking to Hire Veterans

https://www.veterans.gc.ca/en/education-and-jobs/find-new-job/jobs-Veterans/employers-seeking-hire-veterans

The Veterans Affairs Canada website provides resources for connecting prospective employers with Veterans including:

- **Hire A Veteran LinkedIn Group**: Employers can join this group to directly connect with Veterans and post job opportunities

- **Registration Form**: Employers are encouraged to complete a short registration form to help Veterans Affairs Canada get to know them better.

- **Employment & Social Development Canada's Job Bank**: Employers can create a company account with the Job Bank to post job listings and find qualified Veteran candidates.

Government of Canada Job Bank: For Veterans

https://www.jobbank.gc.ca/veterans

- This national database offers job listings, career exploration tools, and job market news to transition Veterans to meaningful careers. They have helped transition military members enter the post-military workforce for over 100 years.

- The career exploration component provides information on occupational outlook, wages, and a skills and knowledge checklist which is particularly useful when working with former military members (https://www.jobbank.gc.ca/career-planning/skills-knowledge). Using the checklist, job seekers can identify their skills from 10 categories and their knowledge from nine areas. Results yield a Skills and Knowledge Profile showing related occupations, skills matches, and knowledge needed. By clicking on the occupations, one can view all the current jobs available by region.

Helmets to Hardhats (H2H)

https://www.helmetstohardhats.ca

Designed to provide opportunities in Canada for anyone who has served, or is currently serving, in the Reserves or Regular Forces. Offers the apprenticeship training required to receive journeyperson status for trades in the building and construction industry.

MasterClass in Hiring: Tap into the Hidden Talent Pool of Canada's Veterans

https://www.centreforcareerinnovation.ca/courses/Hiring-Veterans-MasterClass

- An online course that equips employers with a roadmap for tapping into the hidden talent pool of Canada's Veterans. It has five learning modules that build on the tips and lessons in *The Canadian Guide to Hiring Veterans*, a template for employers to create their own hiring action plan, and a course design that allows employers to choose their own learning path. The MasterClass focuses on shifting organizational culture and capacity, including career management learning, so that employers can find, hire, and retain quality hires.

- When employers complete the MasterClass, they receive a Certificate of Completion, a Veteran Ready badge and toolkit for their marketing materials, and a listing on Challenge Factory's website of Veteran Ready Employers: https://www.centreforcareerinnovation.ca/pages/veteran-ready.

Military Veteran Business Network: Treble Victor Group

https://treblevictor.org

With over 450 members across Canada, Treble Victor is a not-for-profit organization dedicated to helping former military members connect, network, and achieve their full potential in post-service careers. It provides opportunities for networking, mentorship, and professional development and enables Veterans to leverage their military experience and skills within the civilian job market.

RBC

https://diversity.rbc.com/rbc-salute-an-erg-for-military-veterans-reservists-families-and-allies/

As a military-friendly employer, RBC supports Veterans, reservists, and their families through its RBC Salute Employee Resource Group. This group provides networking, mentorship, and career development resources tailored to the unique skills veterans bring to the corporate world. RBC values the leadership, adaptability, and resilience that military experience fosters, offering veterans meaningful roles and a supportive work environment.

Scotiabank Veterans and Reservists Program

https://www.scotiabank.com/careers/en/careers/communities/Veterans-talent-program.html

Scotiabank is a military-friendly employer whose Global Employee Resource Group for Veterans and Reservists offers both groups the opportunity to access careers in the banking sector. Scotiabank believes that the skills, qualifications and professional attitude Veterans and Reservists possess complement those sought within its team. This site also provides testimonials and FAQs.

Shaping Purpose

https://shapingpurpose.com

Shaping Purpose is a 12-hour online course to assist CAF members in preparing to transition to civilian life. It focuses on designing a best-fit career path or next life chapter aligned with the CAF member's gifts, values, and passions.

True Patriot Love Veteran Hub

https://www.Veteranhub.ca/

This hub is a one-stop shop where Veterans, military members, and their families can find volunteering opportunities, events, and services in their local community. It also has options for additional programs/events to be added to the hub, to keep the information as up-to-date as possible.

VAC Career Transition Services (CTS)

https://www.Veterans.gc.ca/en/education-and-jobs/prepare-release/career-transition-services

Veterans Affairs Canada's Career Transition Services provides a comprehensive support system for qualifying and still-serving Canadian Armed Forces members, Veterans, spouses/partners, and survivors. These enhanced services include one-on-one career counseling, resume writing assistance, interview preparation, labour market information, and job search support. Additionally, Veterans Affairs Canada has developed partnerships with employers and organizations to facilitate interviews and networking opportunities for Veterans.

Military Families

These are some of the key services aimed specifically toward supporting military spouses/partners and their families.

Canadian Forces Morale and Welfare Services (CFMWS)*

https://cfmws.ca/

Provides programs and services for CAF members, Veterans and their families in over 33 locations across Canada and overseas.

Military Spouse Employment Initiative (MSEI)*

https://www.canada.ca/en/department-national-defence/corporate/job-opportunities/civilian-jobs/civilian-job-opportunities/military-spouse-employment-initiative.html

Provides military spouses and partners with resources to develop and pursue careers with the federal Public Service. This includes an employment inventory with opportunities across Canada with a range of jobs to look through. Relevant experience, education, work location, and linguistic requirements of the job will be considered when applying for a job through this initiative.

Military Spousal Employment Network (MSEN)*

https://msen.vfairs.com/

This is a free resource for partners/spouses of currently serving and retired CAF members, providing access to employment opportunities, career fairs, and career coaching.

MFS Career Development (virtual career development training)

https://cfmws.ca/support-services/employment/career-development

Offers military spouses and partners free career development training, resources, and other services such as CareerCOACH+, career fairs and events, Helping Entrepreneurs Reach Complete Success (HERCS), LinkedIn content creation, and more.

MFS Newsletter

https://cfmws.us20.list-manage.com/subscribe?u=e04db0cabc23e7bcacad4ffae&id=b296c77230

Sign up for news regarding employment services, events, programs, and career fairs from the MFS Employment Services Team.

MFS Spousal Employment Facebook group

https://www.facebook.com/MFSSpousalEmployment

Military spouses and partners can join this group to learn about regional and national jobs, as well as employment opportunities.

MFS Veteran Family Program

https://cfmws.ca/support-services/releasing/Veteran-family-program

Provides information and services for Veterans and their families as they transition out of the military, including the following:

- **Mental Health First Aid – Veteran Community**, for conversations about mental health within families.
- **COPE: Couples Overcoming PTSD Everyday**, for learning coping skills to manage living with a family member with PTSD.
- **SRP: Spousal Resiliency Program**, specifically for spouses and partners of Veterans who need support managing life with a partner with PTSD.
- **Care for the Caregiver**, to provides resources to assist the caregiver of a medially released military member with an operational stress injury.
- **Family Information Line**, a confidential service offering support to the military community, available 24/7: https://cfmws.ca/support-services/family-information-line.

Relocation Guide

https://cfmws.ca/support-services/moving-housing/guide-to-relocating

Resources for military families to help prepare for relocation, including key dates, checklists, and resources for every aspect of the moving process: house hunting, moving, settling in, finances and budgeting, health care, child care, education, pets, and vehicles. It is a great resource for planning ahead and getting the entire family involved with the relocation.

Together We Stand Foundation

https://www.twsfoundation.ca/

Together We Stand is a national non-profit supporting Canada's military families. It provides programs, care packages, emergency financial aid, and awareness campaigns to educate Canadians about military families' sacrifices and needs.

Veteran Family Journal

https://cfmws.ca/support-services/releasing/Veteran-family-journal

This tool was created by CFMWS to assist medically released Veterans, medically releasing CAF members, and their families in the transition to civilian life. Each section offers guides, resources, and relevant VAC benefits and services. Unique to each family, it also includes sections to keep personal notes, contact information, and reference materials.

Health and Wellness

This list outlines some of the key providers of health and wellness support programs and services for CAF Veterans and their families.

Military Transition Engagement and Partnerships (MTEP)*

https://www.canada.ca/en/department-national-defence/services/benefits-military/transition/mtep.html

- A digital national network for organizations, businesses, and programs that support transitioning military/Veterans and their families. They work in partnership with Veterans Affairs Canada (VAC), Chief of Reserves and Employer Support (CRES), Canadian Forces Morale and Welfare Services (CFMWS), Military Family Services (MFS), and other government entities. To be considered, organizations can submit their details and an MTEP advisor will work with them to consider their application.

- MTEP maintains the **National Resource Directory** (https://military-transition.canada.ca/en/national-resource-directory), where transitioning members search a range of resources by province, domain of well-being and populations served.

Family Information Line

https://cfmws.ca/support-services/family-information-line

A bilingual telephone service available 24/7 for the families of all military personnel, including those who are serving overseas. It provides detailed updates on operations, support and assurance and acts as a complementary service to Military Family Resource Centres.

Family Navigator

http://www.familynavigator.ca

Offers toolkits to support CAF families in managing the challenges that come with military life. Includes support for members in caring for a special needs child, elder care, operational injuries, relocation, navigating mental health services, child care resources, or general information.

Veterans Affairs Canada

https://www.veterans.gc.ca/en/mental-and-physical-health

A variety of health and wellness services are available to support Veterans and their families in areas of mental health, physical health, case management, benefits, and more.

Veteran's Elite Canines

https://www.Veteranselitecanines.ca/

Helps Veterans suffering with mental illnesses to acquire trained service dogs.

Veterans Transition Network

https://www.vtncanada.org

Veterans Transition Network helps CAF and RCMP members and Veterans overcome difficulties transitioning out of service and the psychological impact. Transition courses are offered at two levels. Level 1 is a five-day in-person retreat that aims to empower Veterans and normalize their transition journey. Level 2 is a five-day in-person retreat featuring intensive therapy that helps clients repair their sense of self, rebuild their ability to trust, and restore their values using enactment scenarios.

VETS Canada (Veterans Emergency Transition Services)

https://vetscanada.org/

Seeks out homeless and at-risk Veterans and re-establishes a bond of trust. Helps them move from streets and shelters to affordable housing as well as find suitable employment.

Wounded Warriors Canada

https://www.woundedwarriors.ca

Provides a spectrum of mental health support and care for CAF Veterans, with a special focus on PTSD. Helps any Veteran in need as they transition to civilian life.

Education and Training

This section lists the key providers of services/programs to help CAF transitioning members and Veterans determine and secure the education and training needed to prepare for civilian careers.

Canadian Military, Veteran, and Family Connected Campus Consortium (CMVF3C)*

https://sites.google.com/ualberta.ca/cmvf3c/home

CMVF3C's goal is to be a one-stop shop for all the groups identified in its name to access streamlined educational resources and opportunities. From symposiums, to training resources, consultations, and advocacy, this consortium is committed to easing the educational challenges faced by military members, Veterans, and their families as a result of their time in service. There are currently 49 post-secondary institutions participating (including some of the ones listed below) in addition to a number of other partners.

Algonquin College

https://www.algonquincollege.com/military/family-member-support/

Members of the CAF (Regular and Reserve), Veterans, military families, and DND civilian staff have access to Algonquin College's academic referral services, career samplers for youth ages 12–17, financial aid, student employment services, co-operative education, apprenticeship training, and a Prior

---

Learning Assessment and Recognition (PLAR) process to translate life and work experiences into college credit.

Athabasca University

https://www.athabascau.ca/academic-partnerships/military.html

Athabasca University will accept transfer credits for military experience so that a student can reduce the number of courses required to receive an Athabasca degree. Military members must first apply and be accepted to Athabasca and must have their military experience evaluated by the Military Support Office at the University of Manitoba. The approved credits will, where possible, be applied to the student's program.

British Columbia Institute of Technology (BCIT)
Legion Military Skills Conversion Program

https://www.bcit.ca/legion

The Legion Military Skills Conversion Program is open to both former and current members of the CAF Regular and Reserve Forces plus the National Guard. Enrolled students can fast-track their education by earning BCIT credits in degree/diploma programs such as HR, Operations Management, Business Operations, GIS, Construction, Business Information Technology, and more. They can also prepare for their next employment with the WOWI assessment tool, military-to-civilian skills translations, and job hunting through resumé and cover letter assistance and job boards.

Fanshawe College

https://www.fanshawec.ca/admission-finance/military-connected-campus

Fanshawe has established educational pathways whereby those with military training and experience can obtain prior learning credit based on both the school's and provincial guidelines. This includes individual support from trained staff members, the Civilian Military Leadership Pilot Initiative (CMLPI), apprenticeships through the Military-Connected Student in Trades Pilot Program (MCSTPP), the Millwright Scholarship (in partnership with Helmets to Hardhats), and a fee-deferral program for Veterans receiving the Education Training Benefit.

High School Education Initiative

https://www.canada.ca/en/department-national-defence/services/benefits-military/education-training/high-school.html

The High School Education Initiative (HSEI) aims to increase CAF members' awareness of the importance of obtaining a High School Diploma (HSD) early on in their military careers and is intended to be a guide to aid CAF members in their journey in obtaining it, ideally within the first five years of service. While employed with the CAF, earning a HSD early on in one's career can create opportunities for commissioning plans, occupational transfers, and specialized roles. Additionally, an HSD can facilitate in a member's transition into the civilian workforce or further higher education, when the time arises.

Northern Alberta Institute of Technology (NAIT)

https://www.nait.ca/canadian-forces-program.htm

NAIT has a Canadian Forces Program that allows CAF personnel access to a variety of courses, upgrading options and full-time programs. NAIT grants advance credits to CAF members trained in over 13 distinct occupational areas, including Aerospace Telecommunications, Cook, Marine Engineer, Resource Management Clerk, Weapons Technician, and Military Leadership.

Ottawa Carleton E-School and Canada eSchool

https://www.canadaeschool.ca/admissions/new-students/miltary-families/

Offers internet-based high school courses approved by the Ontario Ministry of Education. Provides for the challenges that secondary-school-age children of military members face due to frequent family relocations, credit transfers, or loss of credits due to differing educational requirements.

Release Point Education

https://releasepointeducation.ca/

Release Point Education offers targeted programs for military-connected students and Veterans, focusing on education and employment pathways. Services include consultations for academic institutions to support military learners and customized hiring solutions for businesses seeking to employ veterans and their families.

Trade Certification

https://www.red-seal.ca/eng/others/dnd_2013_br.4ch.5r.2.shtml

Former CAF military personnel with experience in skilled trades such as plumber, cook, automotive service technician, electrician, carpenter, welder, refrigeration technician, heavy-duty equipment operator, and more can apply to write provincial or territorial exams to receive Red Seal certification. Two examples:

- **Skilled Trades Ontario** (https://www.skilledtradesontario.ca/experienced-workers/canadian-forces/). Offers the conversion of nine military trade qualifications to civilian trade certification (Red Seal). Fees may apply.
- **Saskatchewan Apprenticeship and Trade Certification Commission** (https://www.saskapprenticeship.ca/former-canadian-military-personnel)

University of Alberta

https://www.ualberta.ca/en/current-students/veteran-friendly-campus/index.html

The University of Alberta welcomes Canadian military members and Veterans, offering tailored support through its Military and Veteran Friendly Campus program. This includes an advisory committee, career planning, financial aid, and transition services. Through scholarships, dedicated resources, and a supportive community, the program aims to assist military members in their academic and civilian life adjustments, fostering success and inclusivity.

University of British Colombia, Institute for Veterans Education and Transition (IVET) Program

https://ivet.educ.ubc.ca/

University of British Colombia's IVET program allows military-connected individuals transitioning from services to explore new academic and career opportunities. They provide counselling, training, and educational resources to ensure successful transition to civilian life.

University of Manitoba, Military Support Office

https://umanitoba.ca/student-supports/military-support-office

- Launched in 1974, the University of Manitoba's Military Support Office recognizes and facilitates the training, mobility, and deployment of military personnel. In partnership with DND, the university provides degree credit for specifically evaluated military courses and training; authorizes withdrawals and/or tuition reimbursement if/when military duty conflicts with courses; and provides academic advising and support in response to the educational needs of CAF personnel.

- Military members can enter their Military Occupational Classification (MOC) and their level of training into the university's Military Transfer Credit Form (https://umanitoba.ca/student-supports/military-support-office/transfer-credit-form) to determine (unofficially) if they are eligible for credits. They can submit their Member Personnel Record Resume (MPRR) and transcripts from other post-secondary institutions to receive an official assessment of transfer credits at no cost.

University of New Brunswick (UNB)

https://unb.ca/cel/credit/military/index.html

UNB will assess military training for possible credit to any of its programs. Applicants need to provide their Member Personnel Record Resume (MPRR), course reports for language training, relevant transcripts and course descriptions, a completed UNB application for admission, and pay a fee. UNB also offers Prior Learning Assessment.

University of Ottawa Professional Development Institute

https://pdinstitute.uottawa.ca/PDI/PDI/Programs/Coding-for-Veterans-Program/Coding-for-Veterans-Program.aspx

Coding for Veterans is an online, instructor-led, self-paced retraining program delivered in partnership with the University of Ottawa Professional Development Institute. There are three programs: the Secure Software Development Program, the Network Associate Program, and the Cyber Security Architect Program. These programs are offered both full-time and part-time and can be completed in as little as eight months. Upon completion, students receive an industry-recognized certification and a University of Ottawa Professional Development Certificate.

Knowledge-Building Resources for Non-CAF Service Providers

A wealth of information and resources are now available to help non-military service providers better understand military language, culture, and ethos.

Introduction to the Canadian Armed Forces ("Canadian Armed Forces 101")*

https://www.canada.ca/en/department-national-defence/corporate/reports-publications/transition-materials/transition-assoc-dm/caf-101.html

This provides an overview of the CAF inclusive of its leadership, core mission, organizational structure, and how it interfaces with the Department of National Defence.

CAF Military Occupations

https://forces.ca/en/careers

Describes the various careers available within the CAF and highlights those that are in demand and offering signing bonuses.

CAF Ranks and Appointments

https://www.canada.ca/en/services/defence/caf/military-identity-system/rank-appointment-insignia.html

Learn about CAF ranks, classifications, and acronyms. Note: Ranks in the Navy are equivalent but may be named differently.

CAF Values and Ethos

https://forces.ca/en/values-ethos/

Learn about the values that underpin CAF culture and some of the work being done to achieve lasting change in areas that need strengthening. Targeted areas include employment equity, gender inclusivity, uniform and appearance standards, compassionate leaves, health and wellness, and addressing sexual misconduct.

Duty with Honour: The Profession of Arms in Canada

https://publications.gc.ca/collections/collection_2011/dn-nd/D2-150-2003-1-eng.pdf

This 2003 publication is a seminal work in describing Canada's military history and core culture.

Glossary of Military to Civilian Career Transition Terms

https://community.challengefactory.ca/dictionary/

This glossary provides clear definitions of terms used in military and career development contexts. By increasing access to essential terminology, the glossary helps everyone navigate the complexities of military language and better understand career transition. Note: Funding for the glossary was generously provided by the Government of Ontario's Skills Development Fund as part of the Veteran Friendly Ontario (VFO) project, a multi-tiered collaboration between True Patriot Love and Challenge Factory.

Research/New Initiatives

Ongoing research is vital to the development of appropriate services and programs for CAF Veterans.

Canadian Institute for Military and Veteran Health Research

https://cimvhr.ca

This is a consortium of over 30 Canadian universities actively engaged in research on the health needs of military personnel, Veterans, and their families in order to enhance their lives.

Challenge Factory

https://community.challengefactory.ca/three-research-backed-hiring-resources-for-employers/

Challenge Factory is committed to evidence-based data to facilitate Veteran transition to the workplace. This includes debunking employer misconceptions and increasing understanding of Veteran motivators and behaviours.

Comprehensive Military Family Plan – Research

https://cfmws.ca/about-us/our-impact/
comprehensive-military-family-plan

From this CFMWS web page, download numerous research papers and publications about military families.

Life After Service Studies (LASS)

https://www23.statcan.gc.ca/imdb/p2SV.
pl?Function=getSurvey&Id=1228312

The LASS program of research was designed to further understand the transition from military to civilian life and ultimately improve the health of Veterans in Canada. LASS partners are Veterans Affairs Canada, the Department of National Defence/Canadian Forces Morale and Welfare Services—Publications and Research, and Statistics Canada. Moving forward, CAF and VAC will work with Statistics Canada so that as part of every Census, information will be collected about the Canadian military experience.

Statement by the Prime Minister on Veteran's Week (2023)

https://www.pm.gc.ca/en/news/statements/2023/11/05/
statement-prime-minister-Veterans-week

Prime Minister Justin Trudeau's statement for Veteran's Week (November 5–11, 2023), announced additional resources for Veterans transitioning into civilian life including:

- Veteran and Family Well-Being Fund: https://veterans.gc.ca/en/financial-programs-and-services/funding-programs-organizations/veteran-and-family-well-being-fund

- Accessibility Action Plan 2022-2025: https://www.veterans.gc.ca/en/about-vac/our-values/accessibility-veterans-affairs-canada/accessibility-action-plan-2022-2025

- Gender-based Analysis Plus resources: https://www.canada.ca/en/women-gender-equality/gender-based-analysis-plus/resources.html

"Part of My Life"

Lucy, out of the military now for over two years, says there is definitely an adjustment to civilian life to be made after being in uniform for over 30 years. Her decision to join the CAF was influenced by six years spent with the Air Cadets and the reality that with the CAF, she would be guaranteed a job, get trained, and get to see the world.

Lucy completed basic training and was en route to military college when she changed paths and headed back to northern Ontario to a different degree program at a public university. With no financial support available from her family, Lucy applied for student loans, joined the Reserves and took an additional part-time job, taking an extra year to complete her business degree.

After university, Lucy took on a Class B position on a base, met her husband and then transitioned to a civilian role, as a Mess manager, while maintaining her Reserve status. As a Reservist she was offered the opportunity to deploy to Bosnia and while there completed a component transfer to the Regular Force. Twenty-seven-and-a-half years later Lucy retired from the Regular Force as a Lieutenant-Colonel.

Married to a non-commissioned member (NCM), Lucy relates that this relationship was not always looked upon favourably by peers and superiors and offered its own challenges. As a woman in the CAF there were other challenges to overcome as well. In her last position she reports not feeling supported by senior ranks. It was at this time she made the tough decision to retire, slightly earlier than what had been planned. "I knew it was time so that I wouldn't look back negatively on my time in. I had a great career."

During her many years in the Forces, Lucy and her husband were fortunate to always be posted together, despite moving five times. The fact that they could be posted together (he worked in a portable military trade) helped to keep their family intact and stable. Some of her fondest memories resulted from the ability to travel the world extensively and for which she has some really good stories.

Lucy actually misses the moving around that comes with military life. "I loved the ability to be posted with my family. Staying stable is not in my nature." She also misses the camaraderie and the culture of friends who became family.

Lucy's contract allowed her to provide a 30-day notice of release, so she sought the counsel of friends who had already transitioned out. They shared from their experiences and told her about the services she should be aware of, including the resumé-writing services which she took advantage of. She is now working full-time as a public servant. It is within this role that she faces her biggest adjustment. "I have to match my own clothes now," she says laughing.

Lucy offers these nuggets of wisdom to those looking to transition out.

- ✓ You need to be comfortable with who you are… content with yourself. Nobody is going to tell you. You have to figure that out.
- ✓ Reach out to people who have transitioned. Get a feel for how their experience went before you embark on your journey so you will have an idea of how things are going to go and the resources you need.
- ✓ Don't be afraid to ask questions, and don't pretend you know when you don't.
- ✓ Form bonds with the staff who are helping you in your transition so if needed after you leave, you can easily follow up because of the connection you have already established.

"I loved my time [in the CAF] but it was not my life. It was part of my life."

CHAPTER 13

Conclusion and Learning

This second edition of *Military 2 Civilian Employment: A Career Practitioner's Guide* provides a broad overview of the military-to-civilian-employment transition. Hopefully what came through in the many lists, links, questions, and information is that though the transition can be challenging, it can be managed—with preparation, planning, information, support, and resources.

For the duration of time that a member serves, the CAF provides a team-centric and supportive cocoon where there is a shared purpose and mission. When the member leaves, voluntarily or involuntarily, it is important that career practitioners not overlook how this loss will impact a Veteran's adjustment to civilian life. And while it is true that any individual who has worked in an organization for a long time will require a period of adjustment, it is not often that a group of dissimilar workers will admit to missing the same thing—the shared mission and purpose.

Our profilee Charles reminds us that the culture of the military is very different from most of the private sector, that the military is much more a way of life that transcends the Monday-to-Friday nature of most civilian jobs. "In the military, you got to be part of something bigger. Transitioning members are looking for that same kind of attachment/bigger purpose."

In addition to this sense of purpose, military service gives its members a wealth of opportunities to face and manage challenges. Career practitioners working with military clients can leverage this ability, reminding them, as mentioned by Marcel, That Military Guy, that they've faced challenges before and they can do it again—with support.

The stories of the members featured continue to resonate. They put faces and clothes on the information contained in this guide. It is therefore fitting that we end by giving the last word to Carl, Alberto, Marcel, Lucy, Charles, Blake,

Kevin, and the host of those we will never meet face to face. Their words of advice are repeated here because they bear repeating.

From Carl:

- ✓ Plan early, if you have that luxury.
- ✓ Budget a bit of time every workday as you move toward the end, to do transition planning. It will give you confidence.
- ✓ Become financially literate with respect to your RRSP planning.
- ✓ In your last year of service, plan to live off the equivalent of your retirement income. That will help drive your decision regarding what jobs you can take on after retirement.
- ✓ Disclose any service-related injuries early, even if it is not impacting your day-to-day life. You may be eligible for disability benefits post-service.

Lucy offers these nuggets of wisdom to those looking to transition out:

- ✓ Figure out and learn to get comfortable with who you are outside of the uniform.
- ✓ Reach out to people who have transitioned.
- ✓ Don't be afraid to ask questions, and don't pretend you know when you don't.
- ✓ Form bonds with the staff who are helping you in your transition so if needed after you leave, you can easily follow up because of the connection you have already established.

Charles combined his advice with insights and observations from his life and discussions with his wife:

- ✓ Mindset and attitude are really important.
- ✓ The transition experience is highly personal and very individual. The people who are successful at it are probably the majority of those who leave. voluntarily and are ready to do something else. The ones that really struggle are those who are leaving because they have to, don't want to, or don't know what they are going to do on the other side.
- ✓ Do not take the first job thrown at you. Make sure that it is what you want.

Alberto offers these gems:

- ✓ "You don't want to do it on a whim. You want to be sure you are settled financially and know what you want to do. Plan it in advance."
- ✓ Know when it's time to finally leave.
- ✓ Be ready for things to take longer when you are out of the military.

Marcel reminds transitioning members of two things:

- ✓ The organization will survive without you. At one point you have to take a step back and think about yourself first.
- ✓ Make civilian connections long before you leave.

Kevin's advice to those transitioning:

- ✓ Connect to a new network of support—a team that will energize and empower you.
- ✓ Be honest with people.
- ✓ Have people in your corner with whom you can have real talks and no judgement.
- ✓ Make sure you're not scared of asking for help. "I can't care more about you than you care about yourself."

And Blake, waxing poetic at times, recommends the following:

- ✓ Network. Whether they are Vets or just regular folk, you never know where these connections may lead.
- ✓ Find your new people. Let go of the military so you can take control of your transition, shaping your future with the values brought from the military.
- ✓ Write your own Commander Intent.
- ✓ Allow yourself to grieve. "There's a grieving of loss—lost time, lost friends... allow yourself that time to grieve."

On the whole, our storytellers repeat the key messages that they shared back when the first edition of this guide was written: preparation, perspective and people (networks) facilitate successful military-to-civilian transitions.

But there is a need for something else. Our systems and service delivery methods must not become so bureaucratic that the individual gets lost. As

Charles mentioned in his interview, the current transition experience is very process-driven and a one-size-fits-all system. He thinks a trained advisor at the outset, who can identify which transitioning members are in trouble and will need extra assistance during the process, could do a lot to get them to the point of readiness and making peace with the decision to leave.

And what have we learned from Simone and Dahlia that we can leverage in our work with military spouses/partners?

- ✓ Don't be shy or afraid to ask for help. There are many resources available to military spouses and families.

- ✓ Build a solid resumé/CV where, in addition to skills, perfected qualities like openness, adaptability, willingness to learn, and ability to pivot are highlighted.

- ✓ Consider going back to school or take courses that can help you get a better job.

- ✓ Know yourself and make sure that what you do brings you joy. This will have a big impact on your relationship with your spouse and the people around you.

- ✓ Learn a new language (become bilingual).

- ✓ Start your own business.

Simone further reminds us that a spouse who is supported by the military member and feels respected and appreciated will better manage the inevitable relocations and transitions that come with military life. "They may not have the medals to show for it but they too have done their part."

Transitioning members and their families need service providers who understand where they're coming from, can provide practical support, and can assist with finding jobs and dealing with barriers that stand in the way of that.

That's what career practitioners like us do every day—whether providing services within the CAF or other sectors. That's why our work with transitioning military members and Veterans is so vitally needed. We can help make military-to-civilian-employment transitions happen and happen well!

Appendices

APPENDIX 1

Reflection Exercise

The following questions and activities have been provided by Elaine Piper and are used with permission.

Please note that as certified career development professionals, if you are working with a member who has an operational stress injury, it is important to consult with their mental health professional to determine if this exercise is appropriate for the individual. This and any other exercises and activities you choose may need to be customized to the individual's circumstances.

Reflection is the process of examining your thoughts and feelings. It enables you to revisit your past and current employment experiences and set goals for your future career. Reflection is a critical first step of the career transition process.

The objective of the following questions is to identify the skills you are proficient in and would like to use in your next career, where you see yourself in an organizational structure, as well as the type of organization you would like to work in.

It is best to work on this exercise periodically over a 7-day period, as your subconscious memory will bring experiences to front of mind during the reflection process. Make time each day for quiet reflection to consider the questions.

Once you have completed the assignment, discuss your responses with a qualified career development professional to assist you in processing the information in relation to career planning, decision-making, and job searching.

1. Identify and describe situations throughout your career where **YOU experienced great personal satisfaction**. This can include volunteer and community situations as well as paid employment experiences. The situations only need to be **highly valued by YOU**, and do not need to be recognized by others. If the situations are recognized by others that is okay too.

In your descriptions, please include the following information:

- Your role/job title
- Where it occurred/location
- Time period
- What you did
- What was the result

Example:

- Mayor, Shilo Community Council
- Shilo, MB
- 2019–2022
- Secured funding to double the number of community garden plots. Transferred responsibility for the registration from a community partner to a newly created subcommittee of community residents.
- Increased community engagement of the 565 households in military housing, boosted fresh produce production and healthy lifestyle choices.

2. Make a list of your job titles/roles (starting from the most recent and working backwards).

- Add a column to your list – what you like(d) about the role (in point form).
- Add a column to your list – what you dislike(d) about the role (in point form).
- Consider factors such as the location, work environment, work culture, relationships with co-workers, relationships with superiors/chain of command, assigned tasks, work achievements, and results.
- What trends, if any, do you see in your likes and dislikes? Ideally in your ideal career you want your likes to compose most of the role and your dislikes to be minimized.

Example:

Job Title	Like	Dislike

3. In your performance reviews, in what areas did you receive the highest scores/most positive feedback? Did you enjoy performing those tasks? If so, why? Or if not, why not?

4. When I'm at work, time flies when I'm _____.

5. At work, I am known as the _____.

6. At work, people come to me to ask about _____.

7. What types of tasks, situations, or people "drain" your energy in your current and past positions?

8. What "sets you apart" from others who have your current job title? What comes easy to you that your peers find difficult or challenging?

9. How do you want to position yourself within an organization in your next role? Do you want to be a leader, manager, supervisor, technician, or a general worker?

    a. What are your strengths for this position within an organization?

    b. What are your weaknesses for this position within an organization?

10. What do you consider to be your top 3–5 marketable skills? Provide a brief example of each one. For each example, please include the following information:

    a. Your role/job title

    b. Where it occurred/location

    c. Time period

    d. What you did

    e. What was the result

11. How would you describe your "ideal" position/role?

12. What value do you bring to an organization? What is your superpower?

13. How would you describe the "ideal" organization you would like to work in?

14. Outside of work, what are your hobbies, interests, sports, and/or leisure activities?

Sample Resumé – Military Spouse

Céleste Augustine

Shannon, Qc
☎ : 418 555-5555
✆: celesteaugustine@hotmail.com

PROFESSIONAL PROFILE

- Several years of professional experience in administration and customer service
- Ability to conduct research and prepare reports
- Excellent verbal and written skills as well as a good sense of organizational teamwork;
- Ability to perform administrative tasks and financial transactions accurately;
- Excellent ability to work methodically with precision and attention to detail
- Adept at building positive relationships with co-workers and clients
- Proficient in Microsoft Office Suite, Internet and social media.

EDUCATION & TRAINING

Diploma of Vocational Studies in Hotel Management
Merici College, Québec (2017)

High School Diploma
Polyvalente Le Boisé, Québec (2011)

Client Plus Training, Customer Service National Program
Merici College, Québec (2002)

PROFESSIONAL EXPERIENCE

Administrative Clerk
CHUL Hospital, Québec   2019 to 2020
- Answer and redirect phone calls
- Greet customers, answer their questions and direct them to the right resources
- Schedule, postpone and confirm appointments
- Open and close files
- Respond to requests from physicians
- Photocopy and fax forms
- Manage the appointments schedule of professionals

Secretary-receptionist
Private Medical Clinic, Montréal   2016 to 2018
- Greeted customers, booked and confirmed appointments
- Answered telephone and transferred calls to the appropriate person/department
- Coordinated all email correspondence and followed up in a timely manner
- Entered and classified relevant information in the client files

- Collected, documented and secured payments made by clients
- Developed inventory tables and created a procedures binder for new employees

Recreation attendant

Recreation Complex, Garrison Petawawa   2013 to 2015
- Created a welcoming environment for clients and directed them to appropriate area or person
- Ensured access to the facility and use of equipment and services by authorized clients only
- Provided clients with information regarding the facility, services and range of activities
- Opened and closed the facility in accordance with security regulations
- Addressed minor disputes and referred conflicts between clients to appropriate authority
- Patrolled the facility regularly to ensure rules and regulations are being followed
- Inspected the equipment and facility and report all broken equipment, theft, vandalism, or breaches of security.

Cashier

Canac Marquis Grenier, Québec   2000 to 2012
Grocery store Métro, Québec (part-time)
- Operated cash register and validated payment methods
- Answered the telephone and routed calls
- Filed invoices, balanced cash register and printed cash reports
- Stocked shelves as needed

VOLUNTEERING

Café Découverte committee member for community-based programming
Valcartier Military Family Resources Centre, Shannon, Qc   2023 to 2024

International Women's Day committee member for event planning
Valcartier Military Family Resources Centre, Shannon, Qc   2018 and 2019

REFERENCES WILL BE PROVIDED UPON REQUEST

Source: This resumé sample was generously prepared and provided by Cindy Girard-Grenier and Nathalie Kirouac, Conseillères d'orientation/Guidance Counsellors, Centre de ressources pour les familles militaires Valcartier/Valcartier Military Family Resource Centre.

APPENDIX 3

Sample Resumé – Veteran

MASON CUMMINGS, CD, MISSM

403-556-5556 | Cummings@gmail.com

SECTION HEAD SERVICE DELIVERY MANAGER

A dynamic, innovative, and **strategic leader** with 10+ years of progressive experience as an IT leader implementing systems transformation best practices in the Canadian Armed Forces. Recognized for translating strategic outcomes into tactical action, staff development, and collaborative planning to achieve "**buy in**" from all levels.

- IT Change Management
- Digital Services Optimization
- Information Security & Ethic
- Government Stakeholder Relationship Mgmt.
- Community Partnerships & Outreach
- Strategic Planning & Policy Implementation
- Leadership & Teambuilding
- Human Resources Management
- Cross-functional Communication

EDUCATION

Masters of Information System Security Management, (MISSM) 09/2022 – 05/2024

Concordia University of Edmonton, Alberta, Canada

✔ Awarded the prestigious Alberta Graduate Excellence Scholarship (3.9 GPA), one year's tuition.

Bachelor of Computer Science | Royal Military College | Kingston, Ontario, Canada   2011

PROFESSIONAL DEVELOPMENT

Formal Leadership & Management Training	Expenditure Management	Information Systems Security
Advanced Military IT Management & Theory	Staffing for Managers	Unit Ethics Coordinator Training
IT Infrastructure Library (ITIL) Foundations	Media Awareness	Communications Security Custodian
ITIL Service Lifecycle - Service Operations	Security Awareness	Harassment Prevention & Resolution
ITIL Service Lifecycle - Service Improvement	Safety Management	Presiding Officer Certification

TECHNICAL SKILLS

Software: MS Office | Visio | SharePoint | Axios ASSYST | Service Desk Express | CAF HR Systems

Operating Systems: Windows | Linux | Android | Blackberry **Programming Languages:** Java | C | Assembly

Languages: English | French

EMPLOYMENT HISTORY – Canadian Armed Forces

Information Management Officer 07/2019 – 11/2022
1 Canadian Mechanized Brigade Group Headquarters, Canadian Forces Base Edmonton, Edmonton, AB

Reported to the Chief of Staff for the effective use of IT and IM policy to enable 4500 personnel to work more efficiently. Led a team of 4 personnel providing: SharePoint site management, file storage and information flow; policies and procedures for data entry into myriad systems of record; data analytics and reporting; archival and disposition of records of business value in accordance with the Library and Archives of Canada Act.

- ✔ Interfaced with project team to migrate from shared drives and SharePoint 2010 to 2016 with no disruption to staff.
- ✔ Streamlined SharePoint procedures to reduce staff time spent on superfluous metadata, increased accessibility.
- ✔ Implemented activity-based IM to encourage cross departmental collaboration and discourage plans made in silos.
- ✔ Documented end users' needs and configuration requirements for multiple exercise networks.
- ✔ Selected to represent Canada at ABCANZ IM standards review cycle 2021 alongside the army IMO.
- ✔ Interfaced with development teams on custom HR, GIS, and C2 systems to enable brigade information requirements.

- Collected, documented and secured payments made by clients
- Developed inventory tables and created a procedures binder for new employees

Recreation attendant
Recreation Complex, Garrison Petawawa   2013 to 2015
- Created a welcoming environment for clients and directed them to appropriate area or person
- Ensured access to the facility and use of equipment and services by authorized clients only
- Provided clients with information regarding the facility, services and range of activities
- Opened and closed the facility in accordance with security regulations
- Addressed minor disputes and referred conflicts between clients to appropriate authority
- Patrolled the facility regularly to ensure rules and regulations are being followed
- Inspected the equipment and facility and report all broken equipment, theft, vandalism, or breaches of security.

Cashier
Canac Marquis Grenier, Québec   2000 to 2012
Grocery store Métro, Québec (part-time)
- Operated cash register and validated payment methods
- Answered the telephone and routed calls
- Filed invoices, balanced cash register and printed cash reports
- Stocked shelves as needed

VOLUNTEERING

Café Découverte committee member for community-based programming
Valcartier Military Family Resources Centre, Shannon, Qc   2023 to 2024

International Women's Day committee member for event planning
Valcartier Military Family Resources Centre, Shannon, Qc   2018 and 2019

REFERENCES WILL BE PROVIDED UPON REQUEST

Notes

Readers Guide

[1] "Definition of a Veteran," Veterans Affairs Canada, accessed March 8, 2024, https://www.veterans.gc.ca/en/about-vac/our-values/mandate#definition.

[2] Table 1.2 Enumerated Veterans by Age Group and Gender, Veterans Affairs Canada Statistics – Facts and Figures, updated March 2022, https://www.veterans.gc.ca/en/news-and-media/facts-and-figures/10-demographics.

[3] Mr. Steven Harris, Assistant Deputy Minister, Service Delivery Branch, VAC, providing evidence to the Standing Committee on Veterans Affairs, Meeting 82, February 12, 2024, https://www.ourcommons.ca/documentviewer/en/44-1/ACVA/meeting-82/evidence.

[4] *Our North, Strong and Free: A Renewed Vision for Canada's Defence*, Cat. No. D2-668/2024E-PDF (DND, 2024), p. 29, https://www.canada.ca/content/dam/dnd-mdn/documents/corporate/reports-publications/2024/north-strong-free-2024-v2.pdf.

Introduction

[5] *Strong. Secure. Engaged. Canada's Defence Policy*, Cat. No. D2-386/2017E (DND, 2017), p. 108, https://www.canada.ca/content/dam/dnd-mdn/documents/reports/2018/strong-secure-engaged/canada-defence-policy-report.pdf.

[6] *Department of National Defence and Canadian Armed Forces 2024–25 Departmental Plan*, Cat. No. D3-37E-PDF (DND, 2024), https://www.canada.ca/content/dam/dnd-mdn/documents/corporate/reports-publications/2024/04-22-dp-2024-2025-en.pdf.

[7] Locate your closest Transition Centre: https://military-transition.canada.ca/en/locate-centres.

Veteran Profile

[8] *Strong. Secure. Engaged. Canada's Defence Policy*, Cat. No. D2-386/2017E (DND, 2017), p. 11, https://www.canada.ca/content/dam/dnd-mdn/documents/reports/2018/strong-secure-engaged/canada-defence-policy-report.pdf.

Chapter 1 – Understanding Military Life and Culture

9   "Introduction to the Canadian Armed Forces (CAF 101)," DND, accessed
    September 25, 2023, https://www.canada.ca/en/department-national-defence/
    corporate/reports-publications/transition-materials/transition-mnd-26-
    july-2023/caf-101.html.

10 "Values & Ethos," Canadian Armed Forces, accessed September 9, 2024,
    https://forces.ca/en/values-ethos/.

11 "DAOD 5002-9, University Training Plan for Non-Commissioned
    Members – Regular Force," DND, November 19, 2015, https://www.canada.
    ca/en/department-national-defence/corporate/policies-standards/defence-
    administrative-orders-directives/5000-series/5002/5002-9-university-training-
    plan-for-non-commissioned-members-regular-force.html.

12 "Paid Education," Canadian Armed Forces, https://forces.ca/en/paid-
    education/.

13 "Background," *Seamless Canada Steering Committee Annual Report, June 2022–
    May 2023*, DND, https://www.canada.ca/en/department-national-defence/
    services/benefits-military/pay-pension-benefits/benefits/relocation-travel-
    accommodation/seamless-canada/seamless-canada-annual-report/background.
    html.

14 MPGTG trains approximately 17,000 CAF personnel annually ("Military
    Personnel Generation Training Group," DND, last modified December 22,
    2021, https://www.canada.ca/en/department-national-defence/services/
    benefits-military/education-training/establishments/military-personnel-
    generation-training-group.html). For a listing of other training schools and
    establishments, visit https://www.canada.ca/en/department-national-defence/
    services/benefits-military/education-training/establishments.html.

Chapter 2 – CAF Reservists

15 In 2019 the salary system for Reservists was revised. In addition to their
    base pay, Reservists now receive a percentage that provides compensation
    for additional duties such as overtime or covering for a superior officer. A
    percentage range is included here to better reflect the salary potential. For
    more information, see "Military Pay," DND, https://www.canada.ca/en/
    department-national-defence/services/benefits-military/pay-pension-benefits/
    pay.html.

16 "National Veterans Employment Strategy," https://veterans.gc.ca/en/about-
    vac/what-we-do/service-after-service-national-veterans-employment-strategy/
    national-veterans-employment-strategy.

17 "Correspondence to Employers and Educators of Reservists," https://www.canada.ca/en/department-national-defence/services/canada-reserve-force/information-reservists/reservist-employers-support-services/letters-employers-educators-reservists.html.

18 "Enabling Full-time Capacity through Part-time Service: A New Vision for the Reserve Force," DND, 2023, https://www.canada.ca/en/department-national-defence/corporate/reports-publications/enabling-full-time-capability-through-part-time-service.html.

Chapter 3 – Understanding the Needs

19 "Annex E: Data Details," in *Canadian Armed Forces Retention Strategy*, DND, 2019, fig. 5, https://www.canada.ca/en/department-national-defence/corporate/reports-publications/caf-retention-strategy/annex-e-data-details.html.

20 Hazel Atuel and Carl Castro, "Military cultural competence," Clinical Social Work Journal 46 (2018): 74–82, https://doi.org/10.1007/s10615-018-0651-z.

21 "Longitudinal Qualitative Study on the Health and Well-Being of Military Veterans during Military to Civilian Transition" (Veterans Affairs Canada, 2020), https://www.veterans.gc.ca/en/about-vac/research/research-papers/longitudinal-qualitative-study-health-and-well-being-military-veterans-during-military-civilian.

22 Jill Sweet, Alain Poirier, Teresa Pound, and Linda VanTil, *Well-being of Canadian Regular Force Veterans, Finding from LASS 2019 Survey*, Research Directorate Technical Report, Cat. No. V3-1/7-2020E-PDF (Veterans Affairs Canada, 2020), https://publications.gc.ca/collections/collection_2020/acc-vac/V3-1-7-2020-eng.pdf.

23 "On Guard for Thee: Serving in the Canadian Armed Forces," *The Daily*, Statistics Canada, July 13, 2022, https://www150.statcan.gc.ca/n1/daily-quotidien/220713/dq220713c-eng.htm.

24 Sweet et al., *Well-being of Canadian Regular Force Veterans*, https://publications.gc.ca/collections/collection_2020/acc-vac/V3-1-7-2020-eng.pdf.

25 "National Veterans Employment Strategy," Let's Talk Veterans, accessed July 23, 2024, https://letstalkveterans.ca/national-veterans-employment-strategy.

26 Alain Poirier et al., *Pre- and Post-Release Income of Regular Force Veterans*, https://publications.gc.ca/site/eng/9.897565/publication.html.

27 Mary Beth MacLean, Jacinta Keough, Alain Poirier, Kristopher McKinnon, and Jill Sweet, "Labour Market Outcomes of Veterans," *Journal of Military,*

Veteran and Family Health 5. no. 1(2019): 58–70, https://doi.org/10.3138/jmvfh.2017-0016.

[28] "About the Canadian Armed Forces Transition Group," DND, last modified July 30, 2024, https://www.canada.ca/en/department-national-defence/corporate/reports-publications/transition-guide/about-the-caf-transition-group.html

[29] Sweet et al., *Well-being of Canadian Regular Force Veterans*, https://publications.gc.ca/collections/collection_2020/acc-vac/V3-1-7-2020-eng.pdf.

[30] "Life After Service Survey, 2019," *The Daily*, Statistics Canada, January 16, 2020, https://www150.statcan.gc.ca/n1/en/daily-quotidien/200116/dq200116a-eng.pdf.

[31] At the time of this writing, the course in question, Supporting Military Members in Career Transition, which was designed and facilitated as part of the career practitioner certificate program offered by Dalhousie University's Faculty of Open Learning and Career Development, is currently being redesigned by the Nova Scotia Career Development Association (www.nscda.ca) and will be offered as a fully self-directed eLearning course on their member training portal.

[32] The universality of service or "soldier first" principle simply states that "CAF members are liable to perform general military duties and common defence and security duties, not just the duties of their military occupation or occupation specification. This may include, but is not limited to, the requirement to meet the CAF Common Military Tasks Fitness Evaluation standards, as well as being employable and deployable for general operational duties." ("DAOD 5023-0, Universality of Service," DND, last modified June 24, 2022, https://www.canada.ca/en/department-national-defence/corporate/policies-standards/defence-administrative-orders-directives/5000-series/5023/5023-0-universality-of-service.html.)

[33] "Understanding Mental Health," Veterans Affairs Canada, accessed July 23, 2024, https://www.veterans.gc.ca/en/mental-and-physical-health/mental-health-and-wellness/understanding-mental-health.

Chapter 4 – Understanding Transition

[34] *My Transition Guide*, Version 2.1, CAF TG, https://www.canada.ca/content/dam/dnd-mdn/documents/reports/transition-materials/guides/my-transition-guide.pdf.

[35] "The Domains of Well-Being," Military Transition Engagement and Partnerships, DND, accessed February 17, 2023, https://www.canada.ca/en/

[ ] department-national-defence/services/benefits-military/transition/mtep.html.

36 As noted in a couple of our Veteran profiles, work demands often do not allow for time to be spent preparing for transition. Carl's advice to do a bit each day bears emphasizing with our clients who are in the process of transition.

37 Ian Ruthven, "An Information Behavior Theory of Transition," *Journal of the Association of Information Science and Technology* 73, no 4 (2021): 579–93, https://doi.org/10.1002/asi.24588.

38 Mary L. Anderson and Jane E. Goodman, "From Military to Civilian Life: Applications of Schlossberg's Model for Veterans in Transition," *Career Planning and Adult Development Journal* 30, no. 3 (2014): 40–51. For more information on this approach and on transition in general, see Mary L. Anderson, Jane Goodman, and Nancy K. Schlossberg, *Counseling Adults in Transition: Linking Schlossberg's Theory with Practice in a Diverse World*, 4th ed. (New York: Springer Publishing Company, 2011).

39 Robert C. Reardon, Janet G. Lenz, James P. Smapson, Jr., and Peterson, Gary W. Peterson, *Career Development and Planning: A Comprehensive Approach*. 2nd ed. (Custom Publishing, 2005).

40 Mary Buzzetta, Seth C. W. Hayden, and Katherine Ledwith, "Creating Hope: Assisting Veterans with Job Search Strategies using Cognitive Information Processing Theory," *Journal of Employment Counselling* 54, no. 2 (2017): 63–74, https://doi.org/10.1002/joec.12054.

41 See the MindTools website for an overview of Solution-Focused Coaching: https://www.mindtools.com/axbkkls/solution-focused-coaching.

42 "What is Solution Focused Therapy?" Institute for Solution-Focused Therapy, n.d., https://solutionfocused.net/what-is-solution-focused-therapy/.

43 Shane J. Lopez and Michelle C. Louis, "The Principles of Strengths-Based Education," *Journal of College and Character* 10, no. 4 (2009), https://doi.org/10.2202/1940-1639.1041.

44 Copyright © 2024 Challenge Factory Inc. All Rights Reserved. https://community.challengefactory.ca/legacy-careers-an-answer-to-tight-labour-market-questions/.

Chapter 5 – Becoming Military Cultural Competent

45 Atuel and Castro, "Military Cultural Competence," https://doi.org/10.1007/s10615-018-0651-z.

[46] "Canada's Veterans: By the Numbers," Statistics Canada, November 10, 2023, https://www.statcan.gc.ca/o1/en/plus/4932-canadas-veterans-numbers.

[47] "Service after Service: The National Veterans Employment Strategy," last modified August 21, 2024, https://www.veterans.gc.ca/en/about-vac/our-values/national-veterans-employment-strategy/national-veterans-employment-strategy.

[48] Collins, Sandra, ed., *Embracing Cultural Responsivity and Social Justice: Reshaping Professional Identity in Counselling Psychology*, Counselling Concepts. Available from https://counsellingconcepts.ca/.

[49] "Self Awareness Exercise," Centre for Deployment Psychology, n.d., https://deploymentpsych.org/self-awareness-exercise.

[50] *Culturally Competent Behaviours Checklist*, US Department of Defense, US Department of Veterans Affairs, https://deploymentpsych.org/system/files/member_resource/MCT_M04_Culturally_Competent_Behaviors_final-8oct13.pdf. Note: Though this checklist is aimed at health care providers, I find it relevant for career practitioners.

[51] "The Mental Health Continuum Model," DND, accessed July 13, 2024, https://www.canada.ca/en/department-national-defence/services/benefits-military/health-support/road-to-mental-readiness/mental-health-continuum-model.html.

[52] Atuel and Castro, "Military Cultural Competence," https://doi.org/10.1007/s10615-018-0651-z.

[53] Wilf Flagler, "Acknowledging the Job Loss Emotional Cycle," 2017, https://www.wpboard.ca/hypfiles/uploads/2017/05/JobLossEmotional.pdf.

[54] Robert A. Miles, "Career Counseling Strategies and Challenges for Transitioning Veterans," *Career Planning and Adult Development Journal* 30, no. 3 (2014): 123–35.

Chapter 6 – Finding Employment – The Challenges

[55] Miles, "Career Counseling Strategies and Challenges."

[56] Lisa Taylor, "Research Summary: Veteran Working Style and Civilian Workplace Culture," CERIC blog, June 2018, https://ceric.ca/2018/06/research-summary-veteran-working-style-and-civilian-workplace-culture.

[57] *Career Development in the Canadian Workplace: National Business Survey*, report of survey findings, January 2022, https://ceric.ca/surveys/career-development-

in-the-canadian-workplace-national-business-survey-2021.

Chapter 8 – Education and Training – Needs and Resources

58 Canada, House of Commons, Standing Committee on Veterans Affairs, *National Strategy for Veterans Employment*, 44th Parliament, 1st Session, (October 2023), p. 37, https://www.ourcommons.ca/Content/Committee/441/ACVA/Reports/RP12647997/acvarp12/acvarp12-e.pdf.

59 Veterans Affairs Canada, "Canada Launches First Strategy to Support Veteran Employment," June 28, 2024, https://www.canada.ca/en/veterans-affairs-canada/news/2024/06/canada-launches-first-strategy-to-support-veteran-employment.html.

60 Canadian Association for Prior Learning Assessment: https://capla.ca/

61 Canadian Military, Veteran, and Family Connected Campus Consortium: https://sites.google.com/ualberta.ca/cmvf3c/home

62 These are the rates effective April 1, 2024. For current ETB funding rates, visit https://veterans.gc.ca/en/about-vac/resources/rates#etb.

63 "Education and Training Benefit," Veterans Affairs Canada, https://veterans.gc.ca/en/education-and-jobs/go-back-school/education-and-training-benefit.

Chapter 9 – Recruiting, Onboarding, Benefits, and the Life

64 "Canada's Veterans: By the Numbers," Statistics Canada, November 10, 2023, https://www.statcan.gc.ca/o1/en/plus/4932-canadas-veterans-numbers.

65 Browse for careers in the CAF here: https://forces.ca/en/careers.

66 "DAOD 5002-1, Enrolment, Section 3: Qualifications for Enrolment," DND, last modified June 4, 2018, https://www.canada.ca/en/department-national-defence/corporate/policies-standards/defence-administrative-orders-directives/5000-series/5002/5002-1-enrolment.html#qe.

67 "Co-op and the Canadian Armed Forces," interview with Sgt. Derek Roberts, February 11, 2020, Rogers tv on YouTube, 7:21, https://www.youtube.com/watch?v=eGMYO4nRgdc.

68 "Naval Experience Program," Government of Canada, accessed September 5, 2024, https://www.canada.ca/en/navy/nep.html.

69 "Steps to Join," Canadian Armed Forces, accessed August 24, 2024, https://

forces.ca/en/how-to-join/#st.

[70] "Pay and Benefits: Salary," Canadian Armed Forces, accessed August 20, 2024, https://forces.ca/en/life-in-the-military/#bt. (Note: Figures reflect salaries at the time of this writing.)

[71] "Paid Education," Canadian Armed Forces, accessed July 23, 2024, https://forces.ca/en/paid-education/.

Chapter 10 – Understanding the Needs of Military Spouses and Families

[72] Pierre Daigle, Ombudsman, *On the Homefront: Assessing the Well-Being of Canada's Military Families in the New Millennium,* Special Report to the Minister of National Defence (Ottawa: Office of the National Defence and Canadian Forces Ombudsman, November 2013), accessed July 23, 2024, https://www.canada.ca/content/dam/oodndcf-odnfc/documents/reports-pdf/mf-fm-en.pdf.

[73] Seamless Canada: https://www.canada.ca/en/department-national-defence/services/benefits-military/pay-pension-benefits/benefits/relocation-travel-accommodation/seamless-canada.html

[74] Pierre Daigle, *On the Homefront,* https://www.canada.ca/content/dam/oodndcf-odnfc/documents/reports-pdf/mf-fm-en.pdf.

[75] Zhigang Wang and Lesleigh E. Pullman, "Impact of Military Lifestyle on Employment Status and Income among Female Civilian Spouses of Canadian Armed Forces Members," *Journal of Military, Veteran Family Health* 5 no. S1 (2018): 54–61, https://doi.org/10.3138/jmvfh.5.s1.2018-0026.

[76] *Consultation Paper on the Employment Challenges in Ontario for Military Spouses and Veterans* (Ontario Ministry of Labour, Immigration, Training and Skills Development, 2023), accessed July 23, 2024, https://www.ontariocanada.com/registry/showAttachment.do?postingId=45910&attachmentId=59536.

[77] Pierre Daigle, *On the Homefront,* https://www.canada.ca/content/dam/oodndcf-odnfc/documents/reports-pdf/mf-fm-en.pdf.

[78] Manser, Lynda (2020) "Fast Facts: Canadian Military Families [Info Brief]," *Journal of Military, Veteran and Family Health* 6, no. 1 (May 2020): 13–14, https://doi.org/10.3138/jmvfh-2019-0002.

[79] Lynda Manser, *Relocation Experiences. The Experiences of Military Families with Relocations Due to Postings – Survey Results* (Ottawa, ON: Military Family Services, Canadian Forces Morale and Welfare Services, 2018), https://cfmws.ca/CFMWS/media/images/documents/8.0 About Us/8.1 What We Do/8.1.5.1/research/Relocation-Experiences-Research-Report-May-2018.pdf.

[80] *Military Families and Relocations, Research Synthesis* (Canadian Forces Morale and Welfare Services), https://cfmws.ca/CFMWS/media/images/documents/8.0 About Us/8.1 What We Do/8.1.5.1/research/Relocations-Research-Synthesis-Infographic-August-2018.pdf.

[81] *A Family Guide to the Military Experience*, 2nd ed. (Military Family Services, Canadian Forces Morale and Welfare Services, 2016), p. 17, https://cfmws.ca/CFMWS/media/images/documents/3.0%20Support%20Services/A-Family-Guide-E.pdf.

About the Publisher

This second edition of *Military 2 Civilian Employment: A Career Practitioner's Guide* is published by CERIC, a charitable organization that advances education, research, and advocacy in career counselling and development in order to increase the economic and social well-being of people in Canada.

CERIC funds projects to develop innovative resources that build the knowledge and skills of diverse career and employment professionals. CERIC also hosts Cannexus, Canada's largest annual bilingual career development conference; publishes the country's only peer-reviewed career development journal, *Canadian Journal of Career Development*; and oversees a number of other initiatives. CERIC's activities are funded in large part by The Counselling Foundation of Canada, a family foundation that has actively supported career development and counselling since 1959.

About the Author

Yvonne Rodney is an author, career development practitioner, speaker, and whatever else life throws at her. She has presented extensively at conferences and events on the topics of career, personal and professional development, and spirituality. She is currently navigating what retirement is supposed to look like even as she runs her consulting company, Inner Change Consulting (https://www.innerchangeconsulting.com), and travels where the spirit leads.

Contributors

Organizational Contributors

The following organizations are major contributors to the content of this guide:

- Canadian Armed Forces Career Transition Group
- Military Family Services
- Veterans Affairs Canada
- Challenge Factory

Knowledge Champions

A special thank you to the Knowledge Champions for career development who helped to make possible the publication of this guide.

Athabasca University

Open your options with Canada's online university

Athabasca University is honoured to be working with the Canadian Forces. With credit for military training and previous education, accelerate and progress your career. Explore our offerings and how your military transfer credits could be applied.

Canadian Military, Veteran and Family Connected Campus Consortium (CMVF3C)

The CMVF3C is a coalition of representatives from post-secondary institutions (PSIs), the Canadian Armed Forces (CAF), Veterans Affairs Canada (VAC), and associated partners that equips PSIs to facilitate the academic success of military, Veteran students and their families, and leverage post-secondary education as a key enabler for the public good. https://www.cmvf3c.ca

Fanshawe College

In partnership with the Canadian Armed Forces (CAF), Fanshawe College has created the first-ever Military-Connected Campus (MCC). This initiative provides students, CAF members, Veterans and their families with career opportunities and holistic academic and service supports to help in the transition to academic and civilian life. Learn more at www.fanshawec.ca/military.

RBC Insurance

Protecting you while you protect us. RBC Insurance is committed to helping military personnel and their families thrive with affordable insurance coverage. Visit https://rbcinsurance.com/military today.

Release Point Education

Release Point Education (RPE) promotes academic excellence among learners connected to the Canadian Armed Forces while they pursue post-secondary education. By collaborating with Canadian colleges and universities, RPE develops tailored, relevant, and credible educational programs to address the unique needs of military-connected and Veteran students. https://releasepointeducation.ca/

Together We Stand (TWS) Military Families Foundation

The Together We Stand (TWS) Military Families Foundation is Canada's only national, not-for-profit foundation that puts our Canadian Armed Forces (CAF) military families first. TWS serves these families by honouring their contributions to our country, supporting our services to those needing a hand-up, and educating the civilian population about the pivotal role these families play in our country's overall safety and security. https://www.twsfoundation.ca/

University of Alberta

A founding Canadian Military, Veteran and Family Connected Campus Consortium (CMVF3C) member - proudly welcomes military-connected students to its campus community and provides comprehensive services tailored to the military-connected student experience, including academic transitions and readiness, service navigation, career development, and community connections. https://www.uab.ca/mvfc